SPORTS ECONOMICS FOR NON-ECONOMISTS

This book cuts through the jargon and complicated formulae to focus on the key concepts in sports economics, introducing the fundamentals in a concise and engaging way to give the reader without a background in economics the tools with which to read and apply sports economics in their work.

Full of real-world cases and stories, the book offers a short economic history of sport and explains the economic foundations of the world of sport today, from local leagues to mega-events. Covering both amateur and professional sports, it explores and explains the most important issues in contemporary sports economics, from player transfer markets and the rise of women's sports to the spending behaviour of fans and the growing shadow of corruption.

A fascinating read for any student, researcher or practitioner working in sport, or for the general reader who wants to understand the background to many of the most important stories in sport today, this is the only book on sports economics that you will ever need.

Wray Vamplew is Emeritus Professor of Sports History at the University of Stirling, Scotland, United Kingdom, and Global Professorial Fellow at the University of Edinburgh, Scotland, United Kingdom.

SPORTS ECONOMICS FOR NON-ECONOMISTS

Wray Vamplew

Routledge
Taylor & Francis Group
LONDON AND NEW YORK

Cover image: alphaspirit

First published 2022
by Routledge
4 Park Square, Milton Park, Abingdon, Oxon OX14 4RN

and by Routledge
605 Third Avenue, New York, NY 10158

Routledge is an imprint of the Taylor & Francis Group, an informa business

British Library Cataloguing-in-Publication Data
A catalogue record for this book is available from the British Library

Library of Congress Cataloging-in-Publication Data
Names: Vamplew, Wray, author.
Title: Sports economics for non-economists / Wray Vamplew.
Description: Abingdon, Oxon ; New York, NY : Routledge, 2022. | Includes bibliographical references and index. |
Identifiers: LCCN 2021051947 | ISBN 9780367652579 (hardback) | ISBN 9780367652555 (paperback) | ISBN 9781003128632 (ebook)
Subjects: LCSH: Sports--Economic aspects. | Sports administration.
Classification: LCC GV716 .V36 2022 | DDC 796.06/9--dc23/eng/20211223
LC record available at https://lccn.loc.gov/2021051947

ISBN: 978-0-367-65257-9 (hbk)
ISBN: 978-0-367-65255-5 (pbk)
ISBN: 978-1-003-12863-2 (ebk)

DOI: 10.4324/9781003128632

Typeset in Bembo
by SPi Technologies India Pvt Ltd (Straive)

CONTENTS

PREFACE

The focus of this book is the economics of sport, which I define as *the study of the use of scarce resources by producers and consumers of sport.* Sport is more than economics, but economics is vital to the existence of much sport. Elite sport is clearly at an intersection between sport and business (even when winning rather than profit is the primary objective), but sport at all levels needs money for equipment and for venue access: if costs are not covered, sports ventures will not survive. Indeed the coronavirus pandemic (which we look at in Chapter 15) has clearly demonstrated the importance of economics to sport. My intention is that after reading this book, you will appreciate how sport has become a commodity to be bought and sold; understand some basic economic concepts; be aware of the economic aspects to be borne in mind when discussing the playing, watching, or provision of sport; possess the knowledge to critique statements on economic policies relevant to sport; know what questions an economist might ask about particular sports scenarios; and have the ability to grasp the gist of scholarly articles on the economics of sport.

This is not a textbook on the economics of sport. Most of these are full of diagrams, formulae and language appreciated only by the cognoscenti. If I was not trained in economics, I would run a mile from them! Once you have been indoctrinated into supply and demand curves, shifts in them become a shorthand visual explanation of changes in the markets for sport which eliminates the need for a paragraph of text outlining what has happened, but the latter might be more acceptable to the non-economist. Hence this is a book that will be mainly text, deliberately non-mathematical, informative, and, hopefully, as entertaining as economics can be.

It is not a book of original personal research, though occasionally I will interject commentary on some topics. All the information presented is known but brought together in an understandable form for those who despair of explanations rooted in mathematics, formulae, and graphs. I have supplied references for each chapter, not so much to give the book an aura of academic respectability but so disbelieving readers can check that I have not made everything up; though they are cautioned that the works cited do contain the dreaded mathematics, formulae, and graphs. I hope my sports economist friends (I do have some) will forgive my criticisms, comments, and lack of nuance in presenting their arguments. I admire and respect their work, but this book, as the title makes clear, is not for them.

In fact, this is not the title I wanted for the book. I began with the working title *Sports Economics for My Daughter*. Let me elucidate. Several decades ago, my daughter raised her predicted score in the South Australia Matriculation Maths paper from 50% to 75% after a short but intensive tutorial session with her father. A similar (or even better) upgrading of your skills and knowledge in sports economics is the objective of this book. She said, though it may have been filial flattery, that I could simplify the complex and make the complicated understandable. You will be the judge of that.

Wray Vamplew
Edinburgh, October 2021

ACKNOWLEDGEMENTS

I am grateful to the many colleagues in online seminars and interchanges who have critiqued my ideas: to Doug Munro who has fed me information on Australia and New Zealand and to sports economists worldwide for pursuing their subject.

1

THE SPORTS BUSINESS IS DIFFERENT

Is the Business of Sport Different from 'Real' Business?

Much of the economics associated with sport is conventional. Funds have to be raised, wages have to be paid, and resources have to be allocated to the production process. Yet in some respects, sport and spectator sport particularly have peculiar economics.

In my first degree, I majored in economics and economic history. My PhD was an econometric history of the Scottish railways, but then I turned to sports history and discovered that the economics I had been using did not readily apply to this new field of interest. This was in the early 1970s, coincident with the emergence of sports economics as a subdiscipline of mainstream economics. What became clear as I pursued my own studies and read what the sports economists were publishing, was that in many instances, the sports business and what I will term conventional business were different creatures.

When I did my degree, the whole basis of microeconomics – the study of the firm – was centred around the idea that firms sought to maximise profits. This I soon discovered did not always apply to the particular sports industry which I was examining: horseracing. Owners often possessed racehorses as a status symbol; the horses were consumption goods rather than profit-oriented investments. Then, as I began to investigate football (soccer) and cricket clubs, I found that they too were often motivated by forces other than profit. This led to me contributing historical evidence to the development of *utility theory* in which winning in sport is deemed more important than making money. I found that county cricket clubs were dependent on the distribution of revenue from tests to keep themselves afloat, most soccer clubs were in debt, and horseracing existed only because owners were prepared to treat it as a hobby rather than a business. Little seems to have changed!

DOI: 10.4324/9781003128632-1

Now you might ask, 'Doesn't winning lead to larger crowds, greater revenue, and profit?' The answer is 'not always'. In fact, the two objectives can require different economic behaviours. *Profit-maximisers* are well aware that *profit is determined not by revenue but by revenue minus costs*. However, *utility seekers*, those looking for cups and championships (or sometimes just beating local rivals and gaining bragging rights), will be willing to spend all (or most of) their income to improve the team, leaving little surplus for distribution to owners or shareholders. Although sports economists have tended to prefer the term *utility*, a few have preferred the concept of *satisficing* behaviour, which infers that profit-maximising is not the aim of the enterprise. Hence in the case of sport, it might cover utility objectives but also revenue-maximisation or profit-seeking within limits set by other ambitions. Yet utility-maximisers cannot all achieve their aims. Every firm can be a winner in an economic boom, whereas there can be only one champion, only one gold medallist.

Another significant difference is that while most manufacturers in the non-sport world sell the certainty of their output as being reliable, the uncertainty of the result is a bedrock of sport. Sport is a product whose result or quality cannot be guaranteed: there is no script, no template, and no identical replication. Indeed, uncertainty is the selling point of the sport product, and a maxim of many sports economists is that the more unpredictable a contest the greater the attendance is likely to be. This brings in two related, and often conflated, sports economic concepts: *uncertainty of outcome* and *competitive balance*. Uncertainty of outcome generally refers to the potential result of any individual match within a league or tournament and, by extension, to the competition as a whole; whereas competitive balance is usually considered as having teams or competitors of equal playing ability or handicapped in some way as to render their abilities more equal. We will return to these concepts in Chapter 9.

A further difference between sport and conventional business relates to *monopolistic* and *monopsonic* behaviour in which a single seller or a single buyer dominates the market. Becoming a monopoly is not an objective for clubs or individuals in sport, whereas in the business world, a firm can prosper if it can eliminate all competition and become a monopoly supplier, as this will allow it to raise prices and increase profits. Such a position in the sporting world would be self-defeating since, unlike in conventional business, firms and individuals in the sports industry need a competitor before a saleable product is available. As Walter Neale, a pioneer in sports economics, remarked, '[I]t is no good being heavyweight champion of the world if you have no one to fight' (Neale 1964). He coined the term *product-joint* in contradistinction to the *joint product* that economic textbooks mention when (say) crude oil is processed to make petrol, lubricants, or asphalt or when milk is used to obtain butter, cheese, and cream. No other form of commerce requires rivals to work together to produce a saleable product.

Leagues often operate as cartels, something generally illegal today for conventional businesses in order to prevent them from fixing prices and restricting competition. Yet this is precisely what has happened in most professional team sports. The sports industry has a history of regulations, determined by leagues, which have impacted the free movement of labour and not allowed employees to choose where they want to work or for whom. *Equality of competition* has been promoted by weakening the stronger teams and strengthening the weaker ones by such methods as salary caps, reverse-order drafts, and various forms of revenue redistribution. Moreover, the leagues can impose restrictions on new entrants to the sports industry. In other businesses, if you can raise sufficient start-up funds, you can become a new bank, an oil company, or whatever, but in sport, your application to join a league can just be refused, or you may have to join at the lowest level of the pyramid in a promotion/relegation system. Moreover, in no other labour market can employers collectively impose restrictions on payment to workers, as giving teams exclusive property rights to the *human capital* (see Chapter 5) of their labour force is illegal in most economic activities.

A final difference is that, whereas conventional business can often respond immediately to market signals by increasing or decreasing output, most sports leagues operate on a fixed supply schedule in the short to medium term as league size (and hence the number of matches) is determined for a season at a time. Upwards expansion in terms of tickets sold can also be restricted by stadium capacity, though this also applies to normal firms that wish to build new production capacity.

The Americans Are Different

The standard model of American sport is different from the European version (van Bottenburg 2011) with the caveat that both are different from the European model that developed in the former communist bloc. As a sweeping generalisation, European sport has developed in a different way to that in the United States. America developed basketball, baseball, ice hockey, and its own version of football, whereas virtually all Europeans have kicked a soccer ball and others have made tennis, gymnastics, and cycling significant participant and spectator sports. The development of these sports was organised in different contexts. Again to generalise, schools, colleges, and universities were paramount in the United States, while in Europe the major role was taken by voluntary clubs and associations. There will be exceptions to all these statements. Some sports, like tennis and golf, are played everywhere; America does have voluntary clubs and non-profit-oriented sports bodies, but they don't have the significant influence that they have in Europe; finally, Europe is a collection of nations, many of whom had their own sporting characteristics.

As a basic generalisation, American professional sports teams have making money as their primary objective, whereas in Europe owners were consumers seeking utility from their spending rather than profit-seeking entrepreneurs. The literature on North American sports has tended to de-emphasise utility-maximisation on the grounds that there is no evidence that owners have received less than a market return on their investment, and generally, they make capital gains when they dispose of a franchise. Even poorly performing teams can make profits and few US teams make losses in any season. In contrast, few professional teams in Europe make consistent profits and instead rely on benefactors (wealthy individuals or supporters groups) to keep them afloat so that they can focus on winning cups and championships, gaining promotions, and avoiding relegations (Szymanski 2004, 2006; Sloane 2006). In neither case does this infer homogeneity in the club structures, just an overarching motivation. American sports were commercialised and professionalised earlier and more thoroughly than in Europe, which had consequences for the way in which they were operated. Given their commercial proclivity, it is no surprise that to protect their investments, American team owners opted for their leagues to be closed institutions of competing franchises in which the sole quality control mechanism was gate-money. In contrast, meritocracy was the key feature of European leagues, which were generally open ones in which teams were promoted or relegated between divisions.

A significant difference between European sport and that of North America has been the development of pan-national team sport competitions. Entry to these comes from performing better than other clubs in their domestic leagues and cups, of which there is a plurality at the elite level across Europe. Despite discussions, there are, as yet, few European-wide leagues in sports, but there are several knock-out cup competitions. These European-wide competitions are additional (and significant) revenue generators for the clubs, giving them an added incentive to strive to win. In North America, there is some interchange between Canada and the United States, but only within the context of existing leagues. Generally, the American leagues have remained national in orientation without any international regulatory bodies. This has sometimes led to competing leagues in the same sport, something relatively unknown in Europe with basketball a notable exception (Szymanski 2004). Additionally, North American leagues are generally run centrally by a decision-making body in which all club owners participate, whereas, for example, UEFA, a non-profit federation, runs the pan-European soccer competitions independently of full club representation.

Among other differences which will be discussed in more detail later in the book are as follows:

- Americans punish success (via the reverse-order draft) while Europeans punish failure (via relegation).
- Americans pursue the drafting and trading of players rather than a monetary transfer system.
- American leagues operate on a franchise system with territorial exclusivity granted so as to protect the investment of the owners, whereas Europe has larger leagues with several cities having more than one team. In America, this only applies in major metropolitan areas such as New York, Chicago, San Francisco, and Los Angeles.
- With very few exceptions professional sports teams in North America are privately held businesses that do not issue shares on the stock exchange. None are operated by clubs or supporter groups, as is common in Europe.
- American clubs own teams in minor leagues so that in effect promotion and relegation applies to players not the clubs.
- Revenue sharing is more common in North America, whereas in European football, for example, the only centralised sharing comes from television revenues and with no implication of equal shares.
- Surprisingly in the land of the free and free enterprise, there is significantly more intervention in the labour market in North America.

Have *globalisation* (Chapter 12) and *hyper-commodification* (Chapter 2) on both sides of the Atlantic led to a convergence of the two models? Certainly, European clubs have sought to learn merchandising lessons from their American counterparts, the growing size of television contracts have encouraged equity capital companies to move into franchise sports like Formula 1, and some see the move of American owners into European sport – or, more precisely, British football – as the thin end of the wedge (Nafziger 2008). Things are changing, but have they changed enough to render these models invalid? Closed competitions in team sports have been rejected in Europe (so far) and the franchise principle has not caught on (yet). I wrote this before the short-lived proposal for a cartelised, closed-shop European Super League in soccer. It fell victim to an outraged European soccer public and media, but its proposer has warned that the idea is dormant not defeated.

Public Policy and Political Economy

The sports business does not operate in a political vacuum. Public policy can involve exemptions from the law (consumer and trade practices) and often substantial levels of public funding. Governments can influence sport through their ideologies: because they want to demonstrate the superiority of their system through winning a haul of gold medals, because they want to announce their arrival on the world stage by hosting an international event or to do the same to stimulate economic regeneration, or perhaps because they want a fit and active population able to increase the country's economic output. Sport can also be affected by general government fiscal and monetary regulations, such as the tax they demand from itinerant foreign nationals like professional athletic, tennis, and golf stars, or the decisions to bring in an austerity or an expansionary economic policy. Then there are regulations aimed specifically at sport either to impose a restriction or give sport leeway from rules applied to other businesses. In the interests of profit-maximisation, the US government allows its major team sports leagues to practise pseudo socialism with revenue sharing and reverse-order draft systems while, as part of its strategy for World Cup glory; communist China encourages private investment in its leading soccer teams. In North America, most revenue-sharing schemes have not been challenged in the courts, though the collective selling of broadcasting rights, which was deemed anti-competitive by the courts, was exempted by Congress from anti-trust law. In Europe, redistributive arrangements have been encouraged by the European Commission with the aim of maintaining competitive balance and allowing the professional leagues to aid the amateur game (Szymanski and Késenne 2004).

Essentially, towards the close of the twentieth century, there were three prevalent systems of sports financing in operation. At one end there were the fully planned (but not always efficiently organised) sports systems which were state-run and state-financed. At the other end was the United States, where sport is dominated by private, usually profit-seeking, enterprises, and in the middle lies the European model where most funding, especially at the grassroots level, emanates from household and local authority spending with sponsor finance and national government aiding elite sport. Compared with Europe, the American government scarcely influenced the development of the sporting organisation, function, or culture, and the government takes no overall responsibility for sport at either state or federal level. Sports in the United States were market-driven and developed independently of the state, while in Europe, especially after World War Two, governments increasingly intervened in the sporting realm. Nevertheless, sports businesses, like all businesses, operate in an economic environment that is often determined or strongly influenced by the political ideology of the relevant government. The establishment of the European Union (EU), for example, with a consequent implementation of the free movement of capital, labour, and services across its membership brought significant changes to sport in terms of player mobility and sports ownership.

Two points should be noted. The first is that policies might be secretive rather than overt, especially where rule-breaking is concerned, such as the state-sponsored, performance-enhancing drug programmes of the East Germans during the Cold War period and, more recently, Putin's Russia. Second, the aims of policies can change. Just take China as an example. For most of the period since 1949, when the Peoples Republic of China was established, there has been a policy for mass participation, though its objective has varied. Initially, public sport policy was aimed at strengthening people's physiques and promoting their physical health in an effort to improve the productivity of the population and build a strong national defence force to protect the new regime. Then under Mao's chairmanship, it was seen as a means of social control which would contribute to the consolidation of the party's absolute leadership and enhance the esprit de corps and positive teamwork, which had economic implications. Later, the policy moved on towards equality of opportunity for participation (Xiaolin and Saunders 2019). Impinging on this was a decision from the early 1980s to push resources into winning Olympic medals, gold preferably, to demonstrate that China was an emerging power, economically and politically. The organisation behind all this also changed. By the 1980s, China had established a model of sport development, dependent on state finance and administration. Professional teams were state-owned and managed by sports commissions, which were responsible for funding coaches, players, and facilities. This highly centralised, whole-nation mechanism also had the responsibility for identifying and training potential elite athletes. However, from the early 1990s, China's economic system was transformed from a planned economy to a market-oriented one, with sport being part of the shift. One result of this was a sports sector dominated by the manufacture of sporting equipment, much of it for export (Ma and Jinming 2021). Another was the move into having professional sports teams run by private enterprises, having little recourse to government funding, and having players' salaries determined by market forces (Huang and Zhouxiang 2021).

This book concentrates on sport in market economies, but, as indicated earlier, sport has also existed in planned, command economies. We don't have much material studying the economics of sport in such economies, as modern texts focus on free markets and measure efficiencies relative to that. However, for an interesting discussion of sports economies in transition from planned to free market, see Poupaux and Andreff (2006).

References

Huang, Gangqiang and Lu Zhouxiang (2021), 'The Reform of China's Elite Sports System' in Fan Hong and Lu Zhouxiang (eds.), *The Routledge Handbook of Sport in Asia* (Routledge: Abingdon), 247–255.

Ma, Yang and Zheng Jinming (2021), 'Commercialisation of Sport in China' in Fan Hong and Lu Zhouxiang (eds.), *The Routledge Handbook of Sport in Asia* (Routledge: Abingdon), 238–246.

Nafziger, James A.R. (2008), 'A Comparison of the European and North American Models of Sport Organisation', *International Sport Law Journal* 7.3–4, 100–108.

Neale, Walter C. (1964), 'The Peculiar Economics of Professional Sports: A Contribution to the Theory of the Firm in Sporting Competition and in Market Competition', *Quarterly Journal of Economics* 78.1, 1–14.

Poupaux, Sandrine and Wladimir Andreff (2006), 'The Institutional Dimension of the Sport Economy in Transition Countries' in Milena M. Parent and Trevor Slack (eds.), *International Perspectives on the Management of* Sport (Routledge: Abingdon), 99–124.

Sloane, Peter J. (2006), 'The European Model of Sport' in Wladimir Andreff and Stefan Szymanski (eds.), *Handbook on the Economics of Sport* (Edward Elgar: Cheltenham), 299–303.

Szymanski, Stefan (2004), 'Is there a European Model of Sports?' in Rodney Fort and John Fizel (eds.), *International Sports Economics Comparisons'* (Praeger: Westport, CT), 19–38.

Szymanski, Stefan (2006), 'The Anglo-American Model of Sport' in Wladimir Andreff and Stefan Szymanski (eds.), *Handbook on the Economics of Sport* (Edward Elgar: Cheltenham), 304–307.

Szymanski, Stefan and Stefan Késenne (2004), 'Competitive Balance and Gate Revenue Sharing in Team Sports', *Journal of Industrial Economics* 52.1, 165–177.

van Bottenburg, Maarten (2011), 'Why are the European and American Sports Worlds so Different?' in Alan Tomlinson, Christopher Young and Richard Holt (eds.), *Sport and the Transformation of Modern Europe* (Routledge: Abingdon), 205–225.

Xiaolin, Zhang and John Saunders (2019), 'An Historical Review of Mass Sports Policy Development in China, 1949–2009', *International Journal of the History of Sport* 36.15–16, 1390–1413.

2

OUR TOOL KIT

Theory, Concepts, and Numbers

The Language of Economics

Economists use theory, models, and statistics. Theories provide the basis for generalisation on human economic behaviour; models are generalised or hypothetical descriptions used to analyse or explain something; statistics enable comparisons to be made and answers to be more precise. Yet explaining their use to non-economists has often proven difficult because economists have a language of their own.

One of the dangers of reading economics is that sometimes you will see a technical word that you recognise. Beware. Economists sometimes use words that mean something different to them than to laypersons. When economists talk of efficiency, they are not referring to conversion rates of strikers, runs conceded per hundred balls by bowlers, or home runs per time at bat by baseballers but a situation in which overall satisfaction between all parties involved cannot be improved. One party could do better, but the detriment to the other would outweigh the increase gained by the first. Other examples include the following:

- Investment is not the buying of stocks and shares but the creation of productive capacity. So the buying of a franchise by a new owner is not an investment but simply a transfer of assets. More akin to investment is the financing of a new stadium with room for extra spectators or the purchasing of star players who can improve the team's performance (but not their wages as these are operating costs not capital investment).
- Public goods are not (contrary to what most non-economists might presume) the sporting goods output of nationalised industries or even those sports facilities supplied by the local council. They are commodities that do not have any exclusive use attached to them.

DOI: 10.4324/9781003128632-2

- Exploitation means using land, labour, and capital to produce an output, not necessarily underpaying the owners of these resources for their use.

However, economists often also talk in a convoluted language appreciated only by their peers. Most readers could probably accept that coaches and players are 'input factors into a football production function' (DuMond et al. 2008), but what about Stefan Szymanski's [a friend of mine and a superstar in the economics of sport field] statement that the basis of mainstream economics is

> a model of rational agents seeking to maximise some objective function subject to constraints, which results in a set of demands and supplies for goods and services, which in turn combine in some way to produce an equilibrium .... The nature of this equilibrium is that no-one should believe that he or she could have done better by making an alternative feasible choice, given the choices of others .... This equilibrium (if it exists) is assumed to be the natural focal point toward which behaviour in the real world is likely to converge (a testable hypothesis), and the equilibrium can then be compared with the allocation of resources that would arise if a benevolent and omniscient social planner allocated resources optimally.
>
> (Szymanski 2014)

This is understandable, but it is not easy for the non-economist to grasp at first reading.

But let's be fair. Academic sports economists write for their colleagues and use graphs, algebraic formulae, and insider language, such as marginal factor cost and productive versus allocative efficiency. They should not be castigated for this. Essentially, it is a form of shorthand for the cognoscenti and can be found in all academic disciplines and indeed within sports themselves. Cricket fans use lbw, silly point, and other obscure terminology; soccer supporters know their wingbacks from their sweepers; and baseball aficionados talk of on-base percentages and sacrifice bunts.

The problem is that by writing for their peers, sometimes only their peers can understand what they are saying. Even when you feel that you can understand what economists are saying, you discover that different economists say different things. This should not be an issue. That economists often come to different conclusions is a function of their assumptions and value judgements, the way they have constructed their models, developed their methodology, and dug out their evidence. This is no different from any other social science. What is the truth is contested terrain, as it can be seen from different perspectives, involving diverse interrogations and varying interpretations of the source material.

A final point here is that many economists do the discipline no favours by making the seemingly obvious complicated. For all its good points, did one of the standard textbooks on sports economics need a graph for readers to be aware that positive externalities exist if a winning team boosts neighbourhood morale or negative ones when paying spectators behave as hooligans on their way to a football match (Downward et al. 2011)?

This book will keep things simple.

Theory, Models, and Formulae (but Don't Be Afraid)

I don't want to get bogged down in definitional semantics, so I will simply say that I take theory to be a set of interrelated concepts, definitions, and propositions that present a *systematic* view of events or situations by specifying relations among variables in order to *explain* and *predict* the events or situations. Concepts can be thought of as the building blocks of theory. Models are generalised or hypothetical descriptions used to analyse or explain something. They are oversimplified maps consisting of a few primary variables that can be tracked and measured.

When economists develop theory, they often simplify the scenario to ease comprehension. However, this can lead to an argument by the uninitiated that these theories and models are not relevant to the real sporting world. A prime example is the model of perfect competition in a sports league which assumes that all clubs in the league are identical, that they have the freedom to enter or exit the league, or to offer more or fewer fixtures than other clubs and that all are seeking to maximise profits. On the face of it, such a model bears little relationship to the English Premier League (EPL) or the National Basketball Association (NBA). Some models seem even more unrealistic, such as developing theories based on leagues with only two clubs, or even one (Vrooman 2000; Milanovic 2005)! It makes sense in developing a model, but non-economists might dismiss it as too much of an abstraction. These models are developed because economists, like many social scientists, set up ideal types which may never apply in real life but which nevertheless can help in explaining the actuality. In the case of the perfect competition model, this can help explore what happens when market imperfections distort the ideal type. Indeed, most of this book will be concerned with such situations and will draw upon – in simplified language – what economists have to say.

Nevertheless, some of the models are much more complex and still fail to replicate the real world. There are complex mathematical models explaining how leagues should construct their rewards packages according to how they wish to make a trade-off between a balanced league on one hand and high talent investment and club profits on the other (Dietl et al. 2015). Yet no concrete examples are given, and there is no discussion of how real-life situations impinge on the assumptions made, such as whether clubs are even concerned with prizemoney. No matter how sophisticated the calculations, they are no good if the assumptions are unrealistic and the inputted data unreliable. Sometimes the sophistication outruns the quality of the data inputted. Quite simply, can we trust the attendance figures given for various sports events?

The real problem for many people comes when economists attempt to explain things using formulae and mathematics, graphs and diagrams, (and, of course, specialist language). It is here that economists can really lose their audience.

Look at this formula for explaining why corruption occurs in sport.

$$\begin{aligned} E\left(U^{n}{}_{i}\right) = (1 - p_i)\left[U_i\left(p_j Y - DC_i - POC_i\right) + p_j NPB_i - NOC_i\right] \\ + p_i\left[U_i\left(-F_i - DC_i - POC_i\right) - LR_i - NOC_i\right] \end{aligned}$$

Illicit behaviour will occur when $E(U^{n}{}_{i}) > NPC_i$ (Maennig 2002).

To me, this formula makes sense, but I fully understand why others might not comprehend any of it (apart perhaps for the plus and minus signs). You have to have a particular mindset to follow something like this. For those who want an explanation please turn to Chapter 14.

I promise that this is the last formula you will see in this book.

Perusing a copy of the *Journal of Sports Economics*, readers could be forgiven for believing that they had inadvertently opened a mathematics or statistics publication. Some of the sports issues discussed seem to have little direct relevance to economics and more to do with analysing large data sets (which is a skill of the economist). Do not panic. Let economics nerds do the critique, just focus on the assumptions made and the conclusions drawn. When I was doing econometric history many years ago, my professor said all assumptions should be clearly specified so that others can also make a judgement. He contrasted the open sandwich of good practice with the unfathomable contents of a sausage. Check the culinary expertise of the authors you read. What you can also use your judgement on is how feasible it is to generalise the findings to other situations. Has the test been limited to one nation, one sport, etc.?

The Value of Numbers

And now for the numbers. Sport is full of statistics. Indeed that is one reason why some economists were tempted into sport. Here, especially in professional team sports, was a ready laboratory for testing economic theories on productivity, consumer behaviour, attitudes towards risk, and other topics. Analytics are becoming increasingly used to measure relative player performance, productivity, and market value (Anderson and Sally 2014). There is also no getting away from numbers in sports economics. The simple fact that we often deal with finances and monetary values which, by their nature, are quantitative renders this inevitable. Price indexes (or indices for the more grammatically pedantic) allow for commodities and earnings to be compared in real terms over time. However, there are other reasons for using statistics, such as when growth or decline is being looked at; put simply, larger and smaller are statistical concepts. Numbers can also be used descriptively to set the scene and show the (relative) importance of a particular incident, event, or theme being studied; for example, studies of the environmental impact of golf will be enhanced by a preliminary discussion in statistical terms of the number of golfers, the growth rate in participation, and the consequent rise in demand for golf facilities. Measurement is crucial for comparisons. I have always advised researchers to consider comparative work and to look at other sports, other venues, other countries so that they can put their own case study into context and distinguish what is specific and unique from what is general. Associated with comparison is the issue of perspective, of putting something to do with sport in the context of non-sporting matters so that its relative importance can be gauged. Szymanski notes that the cost of staging the 2004 summer Olympics was in the region of $20–$40 billion, equal to about one-twentieth of 1% of annual global *gross domestic product* (GDP; a measure of a nation's economic output) and substantially less than the $2,000 billion required to bail out US banks in 2009 (Szymanski 2007). Additionally, a great contribution of quantification is to help distinguish between the typical and the outlier, to prevent one unusual instance being considered normal and used to justify a line of action. Essentially, I believe that numbers can add strength to an argument by providing a statistical basis for assertions: measurement can allow economists to be more precise in their answers and go beyond gut feelings and impressions.

However, some words of caution. Statistical analysis is only as good as the statistics employed. They have to be evaluated for rigour and validity like any other source of evidence. It is poor practice to simply use any statistical information without assessing its veracity and what its employment could bring to any argument. Numbers are only useful if those collecting or applying them know what they are doing. Statistics are often misused because the applier has an insufficient understanding of the mechanics of statistical calculations. Too many users are seduced by the sophistication of statistical software packages and offer results to two or three decimal places. This is nonsense unless the inputted data were perfect. Less numerate readers should also be warned that small numerical differences may not be significant to the conclusion of any debate.

Our Tool Kit

So how are we going to approach sports economics? The aim is to offer simplified and understandable economics.

Although I accept the bulk of the tenets on economics in sport, I will challenge some of the conventional wisdom in the subject, for example, by expanding the definitions of what is a sports entrepreneur and the sports product he or she is marketing. I will also present some less strict definitions of economic terms and concepts so as to make them easier to grasp. I am not trying to rewrite the economics of sport, just make it more understandable to the uninitiated. I am not criticising sports economists for what they do in terms of its analysis and insight, but in how they communicate that and its results to a lay audience. Economics need not be as incomprehensible as it often appears. Writers such as Britain's Tim Harford (*The Undercover Economist*) and, in the United States, Steven Levitt and Stephen Dubner (*Freakonomics*) have made economics both interesting and understandable to a wide readership. This author lacks the literary skills to replicate their communication expertise, but he intends to cut through the academic jargon and offer explanations devoid of formulae and graphs of theoretical models.

I will bring in economic concepts when we need them as we go along. They cannot really be avoided, as they are part of the day-to-day operating language of sports economics. However, I think concepts are better understood if illustrated by examples. Additionally, I will summarise major theoretical applications, research findings, and recent economic issues in sport. Whilst acknowledging that although four out of every three non-economists may have difficulty with statistics, nevertheless we are going to use numbers which enable us to get beyond impressions, assertions, and subjective judgements and provide more precision in our answers to economic issues.

The innovative aspect of this book is the eschewing of the conventional economic approach, along with its graphs, formulae, and diagrams. I believe that what makes non-economists' minds go blank is the use of economic theory and economic terminology. We can deal with these and then turn to what might interest them more, applied sports economics – i.e. what happens in the sporting world when economics gets involved. We will look at real-world situations and how economics impacts on sport and sporting events. One trait of economists that I admire is their willingness to generalise as they search for laws to explain human behaviour. We too will generalise as much as possible and not deviate into discussions of outliers and isolated occurrences.

Imperfect Markets and Imperfect People

Throughout this book, I will make reference to *economic welfare*, usually in regard to a group of consumers or producers whom I feel may benefit or lose out from a particular economic decision. The standard economic approach is to argue that *economic welfare* is maximised when *economic efficiency* is also maximised. This is the point at which neither consumers nor producers can increase their utility without detrimentally affecting the economic welfare of the other party. Welfare is maximised in the sense that no resources can be reallocated to make one individual better off without making at least one individual worse off. In practice, this theoretical position on how the allocation of economic goods and resources determines the overall well-being of society is assessed using tools such as *cost-benefit analysis* which assumes that *utility gains and losses* can be expressed in money terms. Some economists, however, believe this ignores some aspects of social welfare which cannot be measured in a money sense, such as a sense of fairness, human rights, and justice, which are inherently subjective. Hence markets that are efficient do not necessarily achieve the greatest social good. This has relevance to sport, for instance, in whether it should be supplied free of charge in schools, the most appropriate distribution of prize money in tournaments, and planning decisions on the building of golf courses that affect the habitat of rare flora or fauna. We then enter the area of personal preferences and discussions on whether everyone's preferences should get equal weighting.

Much of the economics that we look at in this book are based on a free-market economy in which individuals exercise rational decision-making in an attempt to achieve maximum personal utility, be this in terms of financial or psychic income. In turn, their collective response allows us to make statements about aggregated economic behaviour. Such a view of the world is being challenged by behavioural economists who, in seeking to understand the factors that shape and influence behaviour, integrate lessons from psychology with the 'laws' of economics. Their premise is that behaviour is not always driven by a conscious cost-benefit approach to every action but can be influenced by emotional, cultural, or other factors which can lead to decisions which contradict economic theory, are irrational and inconsistent, and may not always be in the individual's best interests. An example is that if you have already paid for a ticket to the stadium, but then the weather turns bad or you feel slightly indisposed, a decision to attend should not be based on the fact that you have already outlaid the money on a ticket. In economic terms, this is a *sunk cost* that has already been incurred and cannot be recovered. This money has gone whether or not you go to the game. It therefore should not be a factor in your decision on the day. It is irrational to use irrecoverable costs as a rationale for making a present decision. If we acted rationally, only future costs and benefits would be taken into account, because regardless of what we have already invested, we will not get it back whether or not we follow through on the decision. For a highly readable view on this, see the comparison of homo economicus and Homer Simpson in Corr and Plagnol (2019).

References

Anderson, Chris and David Sally (2014), *The Numbers Game* (Penguin: London).

Corr, Philip and Anke Plagnol (2019), *Behavioral Economics: The Basics* (Routledge: Abingdon).

Dietl, Helmut, Martin Grossmann, Andreas Helftl and Markus Lang (2015), 'Spillovers in Sports Leagues with Promotion and Relegation', *Scottish Journal of Political Economy* 62.1, 59–74.

Downward, Paul, Alistair Dawson and Trudo Dejonghe (2011), *Sports Economics: Theory, Evidence and Policy* (Routledge: Abingdon).

DuMond, J. Michael, Allen K. Lynch and Jennifer Platania (2008), 'An Economic Model of the College Football Recruiting Process', *Journal of Sports Economics* 9.1, 67–87.

Maennig, Wolfgang (2002), 'On the Economics of Doping and Corruption', *Journal of Sports Economics* 3.1, 61–89.

Milanovic, Branko (2005), 'Globalization and Goals: Does Soccer Show the Way?', *Review of International Political Economy* 12.5, 829–850

Szymanski, Stefan (2007), 'Economists and Sports History', *Journal of Sport History* 37.1, 71–82.

Szymanski, Stefan (2014), 'Economics and Sport' in Joseph Maguire (ed.), *Social Sciences in Sport* (Human Kinetics: Champaign), 165–190.

Vrooman, John (2000), 'The Economics of American Sports Leagues', *Scottish Journal of Political Economy* 47.4, 364–398.

3

COMMODIFICATION

Has Money Ruined Sport?

Introduction

As I said in my preface, economics is the study of the use of scarce resources by both producers and consumers of sport. Given that resources are limited, these individuals have to make choices as to what sports they can afford the time and money to play or watch, what methods of production to use, and what quality of output to aim for.

The Sporting Product

All readers will know what sport is (otherwise I doubt you would be looking at this book) but what is it for purposes of economic analysis? Here we have to treat sport as a *commodity*. This occurs when consumers are willing to pay to play or watch it. Essentially, it can be seen as a tripartite commodity comprising *player sports products*, *spectator sports products*, and *associated sports products* (Vamplew 2018a). Let's elaborate on this.

The *player product* can be divided into five categories of games, equipment and costumes, instruction and assistance, facilities, and clubs. To become a product, the game requires formalisation by the introduction of rules so that participants know what is permitted and what is prohibited. Another form of game product comes with the organisation of cups and league competitions with the players as the focus rather than the spectators; hence, they are usually at the grassroots level. Costume is less necessary, except as an identifier between opponents, but it also serves to show status and demonstrate conspicuous consumption. Modern sportswear can be as much about leisurewear style as practical advantage in the arena: football shirts can send signals about a player's biometrics to the coaching staff, but they also serve in a cross-generational market as replica products that can be worn on non-match days. Instruction and assistance come as goods (manuals, rule books, and performance-enabling and -enhancing substances) and services (coaching, teaching,

DOI: 10.4324/9781003128632-3

and scientific advice). Having somewhere to play is as essential as having the equipment. Commercial operators have generally responded to demand, and the public sector has also supplied facilities, including swimming pools, golf courses, and sports pitches, to promote the health of their citizens and to attract visitors to resort towns. Sports clubs began to enable people with a common sporting purpose to come together. They provided a basis for agreeing on common rules and regulations, created a framework for competitive interaction, and secured a location for participation. They are now a key and ubiquitous institution, the basic unit of much grassroots sport and the site of much voluntary activity, especially for men.

While the market focus of the entrepreneurs in the player product sector is participatory sport, in contrast, suppliers of *spectator products* are marketing to those who watch sport, either at the venue or increasingly on television or other electronic devices. The dominant product unsurprisingly is elite sports matches and tournaments. Spectator products can be increased in the aggregate by developing new competitions, as in cricket where the Indian Cricket Board created the Indian Premier League or potentially in the rugby union where a franchised, international, 12-a-side venture is on the drawing board. Other mechanisms to do this include expanding the number of teams in a competition (and, hence, the number of games) or the season can be lengthened by the use of play-off games to determine champions, promotions, and relegations.

Marketed to both or either of the player product and spectator product purchasers are *associated sports products*. These are goods and services that have been allied with sport in some way but that are not really necessary to the playing or watching of sport, though they can heighten the enjoyment. Consuming food and drink at a sports venue is a case in point. Wimbledon tennis fortnight is the largest sporting catering operation in Europe, employing around 2,000 staff to prepare and serve meals and drinks. Other associated products include specialised sports newspapers and magazines, the 'heritage' presented by sports museums, and club-branded merchandise other than equipment and costumes. Innovation in the associated product area requires an ability to link the product with sport in some way. At times, this has involved lateral thinking going way beyond the replica shirts to include school bags, toys, watches, and fragrances or alcohol. Indeed, merchandising has become the main by-product of football club operations in an attempt to further capture the utility of their fans, many of them global supporters who may never attend a game but seek to identify with a team.

The Demand for Sport

No matter what type of sports product we are dealing with, the same basic influences operate on the demand as for any other consumer product. It can be affected by five major variables: *income and wealth*, *prices*, *population*, *time*, and *taste*. First, there are the levels of income and wealth of the potential consumers: generally as incomes and wealth rise, there is more money left over for spending on things other than basic needs. Sport, no matter how strongly sports fans feel about it, is not an essential commodity, but as disposable income rises, so does spending on sports participation and watching, though not for what are labelled *inferior* goods as consumers switch their spending to a better-quality product (such as golfers opting to play with brand-new Titleist balls rather than second-hand ones recovered from water hazards). However, for most *normal* sports products, demand will go up, and in the case of *luxury* goods, defined by their quality, scarcity, and exclusivity, increased income often leads to a higher proportionate increase in demand than occurs with normal goods. This leads us into the area of *conspicuous consumption*, expenditure to demonstrate one's wealth and status rather than any real desire for the good itself. The concern is not with the intrinsic nature of the good but its extrinsic value as displayed to others. The foreign ownership of EPL clubs springs to mind. Another example might be pheasant shooting where the overall cost is almost 40 pounds per bird shot and yet, typically, game dealers pay only 20–30 pence a carcass.

Second, there is the price of the sports product itself. The general rule is that as the price comes down more will be bought, not necessarily by the same individual (unless they have a fetish for collecting tennis racquets) but by sports enthusiasts in aggregate. As an individual (especially if a season ticket holder), you might not attend more games if the price of tickets was reduced. But others, including some who had never attended before, might be tempted. We must also be aware that the price of *substitute* goods can also affect demand and might tempt a sports fan to switch sporting codes or even forsake the pitch for the cinema. A useful concept here is that of *elasticity*, which is the measure of sensitivity of demand in response to a change in another economic factor, such as price or income. Just think of stretching a piece of elastic. A price elastic product is one where a change in price leads to a significant shift in demand. In general, the more substitutes there are for an item, the more elastic demand for it will be. Conversely, an inelastic product is defined as one where a change in price does not significantly impact demand.

In order to maximise sales, sellers often practise *price discrimination*, which means charging a different price to different people for the same good.

- First-degree price discrimination involves charging consumers the maximum price that they are willing to pay, as with auctions for sports broadcasting rights or sporting equipment on eBay.
- Second-degree price discrimination involves charging different prices depending upon the choices of consumers, such as charging more if golfers want to play at the weekend. In Major League Baseball (MLB), an awareness that fans did not value all games equally led to the introduction of variable pricing, with different prices for identical seats at different games and a growth in ticketing revenue of 4.2% (Courty and Davey 2020).
- Third-degree price discrimination, often referred to as *group price discrimination*, involves charging different prices to different groups of people, as when municipally-owned sports facilities offer local residents discounts not available to visitors and sports teams charge different admission prices for adults, children, students, and pensioners.

Another relevant concept is *segmented pricing*, where slightly different products are offered as a means of discriminating between consumers' ability to pay, as with watching the same game from a corporate box or from a seat behind the goals.

Economists use the term *consumer surplus* to refer to how much more the purchaser of a commodity might have been willing to pay above the market price for it. Hence if a ticket to a football match cost £30, but the fan might have been prepared to lay out £50, such was their desire to see the game, then the fan has benefitted to the extent of a consumer surplus of £20. As tickets are rarely individually priced – imagine the logistics of selling 70,000 tickets all at different prices! – clubs and promoters try to tap the consumer surplus by, for example, increasing the price for particular games depending on who the opponents are, making a charge for the right to purchase the same seats next season, demanding amenity fees for premium seating, and charging high prices for concession products.

Demographic factors also have a role, as demand can be affected by population size, location, and age structure: a larger population can mean a greater aggregate demand for sports products, a concentration of people provides a more accessible market, and the demand for different types of sporting activity can be influenced by the age distribution of the populace. A fourth influence is that of time: sport often occurs in specific time slots outside normal working hours. The coming of the Saturday half-day for most workers was a major breakthrough for the mass spectator sports sector. Others who worked on Saturdays secured the mid-week half-day: so no prizes for guessing how football club Sheffield Wednesday got its name.

Finally, there is the question of taste or preferences, the variable that advertisers focus upon. This allows for loyalty to certain clubs, giving them a degree of monopoly power in the local market, the relative quality of the product being offered such as league or cup fixtures rather than friendly matches, and even the choice of the sport to be followed. Why am I a Hibee fan but my wife's family are staunch Jambos [for readers outside Scotland, I am referring to the two Edinburgh football teams of Hibernian and Heart of Midlothian]? Why do I play golf with Ping clubs rather than Callaway? The answer to the latter is that my friend gave me his set when he was forced to give up the game (by his doctor, not his wife!). Talking of golf, it appears that the taste of golfers is towards less challenging courses. A study of 46 public access golf courses in the San Francisco area revealed that every additional water hazard, hill, and cart regulation led to a reduced number of rounds being demanded (Shmanske 1998).

To return to a couple of influences on the demand for sport, time and income are both scarce resources. Most individuals have limited income and restricted leisure time so deciding how to spend them involves trade-offs between working to earn more money to spend on leisure activities and leisure time itself. Here we can introduce the concept of *opportunity cost*, which refers to the next best option available. If a sports fan opts for a week's holiday playing golf, the cost of that is whatever fees of the rounds of golf might be plus the payments for accommodation and travel, whereas the opportunity cost might be the fancy set of clubs that could have been bought from the extra income earned by working rather than going on holiday.

The Supply of Sport

When looking at supply, there is much to be said for a *factor of production* approach which examines the use made of *natural resources (conventionally labelled as land), the labour force, monetary resources, entrepreneurship*, and *technology*. Such a method can be seen as old-fashioned, but it can force us to think about the drivers in the production of sport. There is an old economic adage – buy land; they've stopped making it – which emphasises the fixed nature of this particular economic asset. The supply of the sports labour force is less restricted than that of land and can be increased by demographic change, including population expansion and geographical mobility, and improved via training and skill development, a process referred to as *human capital formation*. More conventional *capital formation* involves investment in facilities to augment sporting output and fundraising to finance such investment. The factors of production outlined earlier are brought together by entrepreneurs. Such sports entrepreneurs could be individuals or corporations investing in sporting facilities for profit but also might embrace sports social entrepreneurs who provide sport for non-profit reasons, such as municipalities building swimming pools to promote health-giving activities or educationalists who encourage sport for its ethical values. Then there is the issue of how the factors were combined, conventionally referred to as technology, partly in the narrow sense of improved equipment and methods but also in a broader concept covering the development of leagues and other competitions.

Let us look a bit more at the first category of technology, leaving the other variety to be discussed in a later chapter. Technological improvement is important in all sports, as it can offer a marginal advantage to those who adopt it first. Some sports, however, are more technologically oriented than others. Formula 1 is a prime example where, every season, new technologies are introduced by a team, appealed against, and ratified, leaving the other teams to play catch up. Sportspersons with apparently perfect bodies (well much better than I ever possessed) have accepted that technology can offer improvements. The eyes have become regarded as another piece of equipment to be changed by technology. Golfers, baseballers, basketballers, and others have had laser surgery to improve on normal eyesight. Scientific knowledge and technology have helped athletes break records by improving not just their bodies but also the environment in which they perform. One estimate is that Jesse Owens, winning Olympian in the 1936 100 metres, who had a best time of 10.2 seconds, would have been only a stride behind Usain Bolt's 2013 World Championship winning time of 9.77 seconds had he had the benefit of a modern track, running shoes, and starting block technology. This, of course, is at the elite level. The diffusion of technological breakthroughs down to the grassroots can be restricted by patents, designed to incentivise innovation by preventing *free riders* eating into the profits of the original designer without bearing the costs of development (Brown 2020).

Like sport itself, sports products can be dynamic and subject to change. Often, this involves the application of technology, but more generally, we can use four concepts to analyse developments on the supply side of sport. *Commercial widening* occurs when more revenue is obtained from traditional gate revenue sources, such as the playing of more games or the expansion of stadium capacity when there is excess demand for the event being sold: in effect a business strategy of 'more of the same'. *Commercial deepening* involves the development of new revenue sources, such as sponsorship, merchandising, signage, and media rights. *Product improvement* involves modifying the original sporting competition so as to attract larger audiences, either for one event or over a season. Such changes include the establishment of new competitions within the sport or the introduction of play-offs for promotion from one division to another. These developments add more events to the sporting calendar but do not change the essence of the traditional game. *Product development*, on the other hand, can drastically change the nature of a sport and the way in which it is played. A prime example is the emergence of 20/20 cricket, a game far removed from the traditional five-day test match or the awarding of three points for a win in Italian football, which changed the nature of Serie A from being highly defensive to a more attacking mode (Alfano et al. 2021).

Characteristics of the Sport Product

There are several distinguishing features of sport as an economic good. It can be *non-durable* and *non-predictable*; function as an *intermediate*, *merit*, or *complementary product*; and be consumed as a *private* or *public good* (Vamplew 2018b).

Unlike many consumables, the spectator product is non-durable. Once played, a game or a match is over and cannot be stored for future consumption (except as a newspaper match report or for replaying on an electronic device, but the result is known and the excitement perhaps dissipated). In contrast, sports equipment producers are concerned with the durability of their goods, which they see as an important selling point: participants want reliability when they purchase a tennis racquet or golf club. Participants also want predictability in that the equipment, club membership, or instruction manual will deliver as stated when purchased. In contrast, spectator products should be non-predictable. They are products whose results should not and whose quality cannot be guaranteed.

Generally, sport is regarded as a consumer good, but sometimes it can be regarded as an intermediate product. It all depends on the motivation of those involved. If you are playing for fun, then sport is a consumer good, but if you are playing to get healthy, sport is a means to an end and thus is an intermediate good. Sport is a merit good when it becomes supplied by the state or public authority because of a shortfall in demand. Remembering that demand is always a demand for a good at a particular price, there could be inadequate demand because potential consumers do not have enough income or, to use the taste variable, don't appreciate the benefits of participation and thus do not rate it highly in their spending priorities. The concept of the merit good is an interesting way of examining school sport: would children have taken part if it had not been made a compulsory activity?

Sport products, spectator ones especially, are often complementary goods. They are rarely sold to the consumer without being in a package with other consumer goods and services. Going to the match can also involve the travel product, the betting product, the catering product, and the alcohol product. Complementarity can have economic consequences, something too often ignored by economists when looking at the *price elasticity of demand* for sports events. They fail to take into account the fact that consumers pay more than just the ticket price of the event itself. The purchasers also have (implicit) time and (actual) travel and other costs to consider when making a decision whether to attend or not. Hence, population migration, transport developments, changing opportunity costs, and the socio-economic status of potential fans can influence attendance. Indeed for the English Premier League, such variables have been more important than the ticket price itself (Feehan et al. 2003). Some aspects of complementary goods are what economists label *derived demand*, which only occurs because of the initial demand to play or watch sport. Another aspect of derived demand is down the supply chain where, for example, historically, the growth of tennis led to a demand for gut from slaughterhouses for use in racquets. Some sports goods have an element of complementarity within them. Playing a round of golf is a prime example of what is termed *indivisibility*. Each course differentiates itself in terms of its yardage, difficulty, the condition of its greens and fairways, but once a player decides on where to play, he or she has to accept the whole package. They cannot elect to pay to play on one course's long holes, another's short ones, and putt on the greens at a third course.

Finally, we have the distinction between *public and private goods*, which is not about who supplies them but whether their use is exclusive (private) or can be enjoyed by many without excluding other users (public). For example, a ticket for the 2020 Super Bowl, in which the Kansas City Chiefs beat the San Francisco 49ers, can be seen as a private good since if bought by one spectator, it is not available for use by another, but the good feeling of winning the cup could be shared by all Kansas City fans, whether or not they were at the match and hence can be considered a public one.

What Do Sports Teams Produce?

Economists have been 'notoriously vague as to what a sports team produces' (Brook 2005). Common sense should dictate that the output is the game that they play; that is what spectators pay their money to see. However, for reasons associated with their specific research topics, sports economists have been reluctant to accept the obvious, with the two most common substitute measures being crowd size and the team's win/loss record (Mason 1999; Brook 2005). Neither seems appropriate. That one game might attract a crowd of 50,000 and another less than 1,000 is a reflection of the perceived quality of the product rather them being different products altogether. Variations in attendance affect a team's revenue stream but do not change the level of team production. The measure of team supply is games, whereas attendance is the measure of consumer demand. If COVID-19 means that games have to be played behind closed doors, does this mean that there is no product? As for winning percentages, if a team lost all its games, theoretically it would have no output despite both sides having contributed to the production of a match. I rest my case. For a more detailed discussion, see Vamplew (2018b).

Market Failures

In a private enterprise system, market failures occur when issues in the exchange process between buyers and sellers prevent markets from efficiently allocating scarce resources to the point where neither the seller nor the consumer can benefit further. Market failures take four forms, respectively, involving *public goods*, *market control*, *externalities*, and *imperfect information*. All of these occur in sports markets.

- Public goods are goods that can be consumed simultaneously by a large number of people without the consumption by one person imposing an *opportunity cost* (the foregone consumption) on others, what is termed *nonrival consumption*. If a stadium is full then, the purchase of the last ticket by one fan excludes another one from attending the game: the match is a *private good*. However, all fans, whether they pay for a ticket or not, can share in the delight of their team's victory: this delight is a public good, as non-ticketholders cannot be excluded from its benefits. Public goods cause inefficiency in economic terms because such *free riders* cannot be excluded from consumption, which then prevents voluntary market exchanges from efficiently allocating resources.
- Limited competition between buyers or between sellers means that the price of the goods or services or the volume of their supply is unduly influenced by one side or the other. Examples in sport include the small number of large buyers in some professional sports leagues and the monopoly position of mega sports championship rights holders like Federation Internationale de Football Association (FIFA) and the International Olympic Committee.
- Externalities prevent efficiency because *external costs or external benefits* mean that demand prices or supply prices do not fully reflect the value of goods produced. An externality exists if a benefit is not included in the demand price or a cost is not included in the supply price. As such, market equilibrium does not achieve an efficient allocation. Training and coaching provide an example of externality. The benefits of such skill transfer education extend beyond those receiving it to include the spectators who see a better-quality product but who do not pay the training fees.
- Market information is often imperfect in that one side has more knowledge about the product than the other, which results in a higher or lower price being paid than would otherwise be the case. Buyers might be willing to pay more (or less) for a good because they don't know the true benefits generated, or sellers might be willing to accept more (or less) for a good than the true *opportunity cost* of production. Wage negotiations in the era before players had agents are a prime example in sport, as is the bidding process to host major events.

Generally, when markets fail to efficiently allocate the production, consumption, or provision of resources, such failures can only be corrected by *government intervention*. This might take the form of direct government provision or production, often done with public goods; or the proposed remedy, especially for market control and imperfect information, might be legislation; while taxes are a method of intervention often used in the case of externalities. However, government intervention does not guarantee that the problem will be solved. Special interest groups can unduly influence government policy (as has been alleged with the ability of baseball teams in the United States to bypass anti-trust legislation); moreover, any policy is dependent on government bureaucracy to enforce it (and we can all cite instances of this not happening).

Has Money Ruined the Game?

Whereas much sport has only a *use value* – its intrinsic worth to the participant – commercialisation gives it an *exchange value* at a price in the marketplace. Once this happens, the profit motive can become paramount. From the 1960s onwards, commercialism in sport began to reach new levels. Media developments helped bring huge new audiences, making sport an attractive proposition for advertisers. Sport today is intimately associated with money, be it the millions spent on Olympic bids, and even more on facilities for hosting the Games; premier league footballers' wage demands; or the telephone numbers inherent in TV sporting contracts. We have now reached a stage that some commentators have labelled *hyper-commodification*. Sport has in their view been penetrated by market forces to an unprecedented extent. As Rosen and Sanderson (2001) put it, '[W]hat was always a business has become a much bigger business, with players' salaries, franchise values and stadium costs all shifted by orders of magnitude': and this was two decades ago! Three key features are usually identified.

- Elite clubs have become organised as corporate bodies in which profits are given higher priority within the (sporting) enterprise over social and cultural considerations. Associated with this is that they have become trans-national identities with fans (or are they now consumers?) drawn from a world market, power resides with large investors, franchises can be shifted, and in some countries, sports clubs can be bought by media interests who may have agendas not congruent with that of the fans.
- Players have become totally professionalised with greater geographical mobility and no longer represent their local communities.
- There has been a proliferation of advertising and merchandising: indeed, some teams have become brands as much as sports clubs.

Although economists have tended to analyse commercialisation in sport without making value judgements, many sports fans are unhappy with a situation in which they believe sport has sold out to business interests. Such objections have rarely been aggregated but include the reduced emphasis on sport for enjoyment and health and a disregard within sport for ethical behaviour. Supporters are now regarded as consumers, and if they cannot afford to attend, then someone will take their place: the working out of free-market forces means that Joe and Josephine Public are being priced out in favour of the 'prawn sandwich' brigade. Then there is television where the money being paid for broadcasting rights has forced sports organisers to agree to change and compromise the timing, location, and even rules of events.

As a person educated in history but trained in economics, let me nail my colours to the mast. Many sports commentators allude to a previous era in particular sports, or sport generally, in which money played a less prominent role than now; in which genuine amateurism prevailed; in which drugs, violence, and corruption were non-existent; and where everyone, both on and off the pitch, 'played the game'. Sports historians have shown that this was never really the case. A longing after an idealised past has more to do with the present and its perceived problems than the real past. It is built on the implicit assumption that the sporting past was a better place in which to play and watch games. It wasn't. As an economist, my response would be to assess the economic welfare stemming from improved stadium facilities and from television offering a better view than the best seats on the ground.

References

Alfano, Vincenzo, Lorenzo Cicatiello, Giuseppe Lucio Gaeta, Michele Gallo and Francesca Rotondo (2021), 'Three Is a Magic Number: Evidence on the Effects of the Application of the Three-Point Rule in Italy's Serie A', *Journal of Sports Economics* 22.3, 329–356.

Brook, Stacey (2005), 'What Do Sports Teams Produce?', *Journal of Economic Issues* 39.3, 792–797.

Brown, James (2020), 'The Creation and Regulation of Sports Equipment: Implications for the Future', *Entertainment and Sports Law Journal* 18.8, 1–11.

Courty, Pascal and Luke Davey (2020), 'The Impact of Variable Pricing, Dynamic Pricing, and Sponsored Secondary Markets in Major League Baseball', *Journal of Sports Economics* 21.2, 115–138.

Feehan, Patrick, David Forrest and Robert Simmons (2003), 'Premier League Soccer: Normal or Inferior Good?', *European Sport Management Quarterly* 3.1, 31–45.

Mason, Daniel S. (1999), 'What Is the Sport Product and Who Buys It? The Marketing of Professional Sports Leagues', *European Journal of Marketing* 33.3/4, 402–409.

Rosen, Sherwin and Allen Sanderson (2001), 'Labour Markets in Professional Sports', *Economic Journal* 111, 47–68.

Shmanske, Stephen (1998), 'Price Discrimination at the Links', *Contemporary Economic Policy* 26, 368–378.

Vamplew, Wray (2018a), 'Products, Promotion and (Possibly) Profits: Sports Entrepreneurship Revisited', *Journal of Sport History* 45.2, 183–201.

Vamplew, Wray (2018b), 'The Commodification of Sport: Exploring the Nature of the Sports Product', *International Journal of the History of Sport* 35.7–8, 659–672.

4

MASS PARTICIPATION, SPORTS CLUBS, AND COMMERCIAL AMATEURISM

Supplying Sport for All

Despite the media emphasis on elite sport, most sport today is still played by amateurs at the recreational level. By amateur we mean someone who does not receive any economic benefit from playing: indeed, the reverse is often the case, and the amateur more often than not actually has to lay out money in order to play, be it a club subscription, costs of travel to the match, or replacing damaged equipment.

In theory, in the free market, *consumer preferences*, including the trade-off between work (income generating) and leisure (income expenditure and income non-accrual), the private sector should provide the desired amount of participatory sport, with government involvement being limited to ensuring that potential sports participants have the requisite information to make informed decisions. In practice, it doesn't always work like that, and there is a mixed economy in the supply of mass participation sport. Yet, apart from a growing involvement at the top end of the leisure, keep-fit market generally and children's sport (specifically in the United States where there are significant profits to be made) private-enterprise, commercialised sport is a minor supplier to the participant market. Most amateur sport comprises unorganised activities such as swimming, cycling, and informal games using facilities available naturally or provided by national or local authorities, though participants do resort to the private sector for their costumes and equipment. The justification of governments to intervene in the sports market is that sport is a good which ought to be consumed in order to improve the health and well-being of the populace. If the prices charged by the private sector are too high to tempt consumers, then subsidies or direct provision can change that price structure. If taste is the problem, then appropriate public-sector advertising might nudge people into becoming sports consumers. Or, if you recall the previous chapter, for true *merit goods* (which people do not want to consume but those in power think they should) there is compulsion,

DOI: 10.4324/9781003128632-4

as with school sport throughout Europe and shopfloor calisthenics in Asia. Lying between the public and private sector are sports clubs, most of which exist on an intermediate point between fully private goods (which can exclude some buyers and are rivalrous in that consumption by one person precludes consumption by another) and fully public goods (which can do neither). They are collectives which people chose to join in order to consume a good, share its production costs, and enjoy the company of like-minded individuals. The club can set entry requirements designed to exclude some aspiring members, but the use of its facilities by one member does not impinge on their use by others until congestion occurs.

Children

Surprisingly in an age of sport for all, there is very little mention of children in any of the main sports economics texts or journals. Yet as children have moved from playing games to becoming sports participants, they have also become a significant consumer group. The US youth sports economy in 2017 was estimated as being a $15.3 billion market (Gregory 2017). The average spending of American families on their children aged 8–18 who played sport in 2016 was $1,150 for basketball, $1,450 (soccer), $2,750 (football), $4,044 (baseball and softball), $7,000 (ice hockey), and $8,000 (lacrosse; the figures have been rounded, as I don't think accuracy to the nearest dollar is warranted). For those whose children played in travel teams (youth sports teams that play at an elite level), the costs would be significantly higher. These teams travel, often long distances and out of state, to games and tournaments and are usually part of a private or club sports programme rather than a recreational league or one affiliated with a school. Some local authorities, who used to try and attract a minor league team to their city, have now opted to construct centres to host travel team tournaments, gambling that the spending of these players and their families will boost the local economy. In 2014, Westfield in Indiana issued $70 million in bonds to build the 400-acre Grand Park Sports Campus, with 31 grass and synthetic sports fields, 26 softball and baseball diamonds, and a 370,000 square foot indoor facility. American youth sport has become privatised as commerce has replaced community. In contrast, is the Balga Soccer Club in Australia. According to data from Sport Australia's 2020 Ausplay survey, families are forking out a median of $600 a year for their kids to participate in sport so, in order not to remove opportunities from low-income families, the Balga club, located in the heart of one of Perth's most disadvantaged areas, has instituted a fee-free programme if parents give their time as volunteers: a win-win situation.

Economics of the Sports Club

Sports clubs are the basic organisational unit in sport worldwide, yet they offer more than sport and perhaps that is their attraction for many people. It is not just conviviality and the creation of social capital but also the binding together of a membership by a community of interest. By facilitating access to sport, clubs can contribute to health and fitness (including reduced obesity) – lifelong depending on the sport – as well as to happiness and well-being; by providing a means for people to meet, they can assist social capital formation, both bonding and bridging, and promote community cohesion, and by encouraging volunteers to assist in club affairs, they help individuals take a positive social role from which they, the club and the community can gain.

Building on the pioneering work of Buchanan, Szymanski propounded an economic theory of the sports club based on individuals making *rational choices* (Buchanan 1965; Szymanski 2010, 71–82). The premise is that participation in sport is generally a voluntary activity. People choose to play sport, and they choose to join sports clubs: there is no compulsion involved. Buchanan's study was the first attempt to develop a formal theoretical structure to cover collective ownership-consumption arrangements. Much of his argument centred on theorising the optimal size of a club which was reached when the marginal benefit of an additional member reducing the subscription costs to individual members equalled the marginal cost brought about by pressure on facilities. His work applied to any institution with cooperative membership, not sports clubs in particular, and did not consider the theoretical problems consequent on many sports clubs having two sets of facilities, one for playing and one for socialising.

Sports clubs are heterogeneous institutions, each supplying consumers with specific tastes for a particular sport, level of competition, and type of sociability in a relatively small market. For a discussion of the definition of a sports club and of the various types, see Vamplew (2013). The concept can include a few profit-seeking enterprises like the American country clubs which are status symbols, statements of exclusivity, and demonstrations of conspicuous consumption, but most are less interested in making profits. So we have multi-sports clubs – common in Europe and often associated with football clubs – with low membership fees to make them accessible to the general public; municipally owned clubs, which are operated for the benefit of local citizens; and the vast majority of clubs, which are membership organisations run in the interests of their members. Such sports clubs lie towards the private good end of the voluntary sector, as they sell services to members for a subscription fee, but they are not profit-maximisers, as they generally seek to cover costs, with any potential surplus used for the benefit of members collectively rather than distributed in the form of dividends. Most clubs also operate in a deliberately restricted market and limit the size of the membership, as well as excluding those which they do not want to join: both these actions reduce potential revenue. Outright private enterprise usually shies away from clubs as it does not anticipate a sufficient level of profit if all costs have to be covered. Government too, like the private sector, prefers a homogeneous demand where a 'one-size-fits-all' policy can be pursued.

Apart from member subscriptions, clubs have three other resources to draw upon: public-sector payments, commercial activity (hospitality, sponsorship, and facility hire), and voluntary labour, which is perhaps the keystone of their ability to function. I cannot recall any of my friends ever offering to sweep the factory floor for free or perform pro bono tasks in the supermarket, but ask them to paint the clubhouse, run the line, or ferry half a team to an away game – no problem. There have been a few attempts, albeit dated, to place a value on this labour voluntarily given. As a proportion of GDP, the estimates ranged from 0.03% in the United Kingdom and 0.1% in Germany to 2.2% in Sweden (Andreff 2006). These calculations necessitated what are termed *shadow wages* to be applied to the volume of unpaid work, itself measured or estimated from various government surveys. Conventionally three types of shadow wage have been utilised:

- The opportunity cost wage (the rate paid to volunteers at their paid job)
- The overall replacement cost using the average hourly rate for private employees
- The replacement cost by activity using industry average wages.

The choice can have significant effects on the final measurement

That members give their labour gratis does not necessarily infer that it has cost them lost income (earnings foregone elsewhere – remember *opportunity cost*), as many volunteers gain psychic income (a notional rather than an actual income stream) from being altruistic. In other words, volunteering contributes to the maximisation of their *utility* (the welfare of individuals as defined by them) by raising their well-being through a feel-good factor of helping others and simultaneously enhancing their social status within the club. One possible future problem is that, if the private sector takes on some of the club activities or the clubs themselves venture further into commercial pursuits, volunteers might become less willing to come forward, thus raising costs for participants and reducing community psychic income and social welfare.

Commercial Amateurism

Until sports went open and Olympic regulations changed, most elite Olympic sports were examples of what the author has termed *commercial amateurism* in which gate-money was charged to watch overtly amateur sportspersons perform (Porter and Vamplew 2018). The last major sport to abandon this organisational structure was rugby union, which shed its distaste of professionalism in 1995. Nevertheless, there are two significant sport sectors where commercial amateurism still holds sway: American college sport and Gaelic sport in Ireland.

Universities worldwide are dedicated to teaching, learning, and research, but in the United States, uniquely, they also host a $16 billion a year sports enterprise. College sport, as it is termed in the United States, has become part of the mass entertainment industry and generates substantial sums from ticket sales, concessions, merchandising, parking, broadcasting contracts, and appearances in post-season competitions (Chudacoff 2015). In 2017, it generated $13 billion, which compared more than favourably with the National Football League (NFL; $14 billion), MLB ($10 billion), and the NBA ($7.4 billion). The average annual total for a football programme is more than $20 million, with teams in the two biggest conferences averaging over $35 million in revenue and close to $20 million in football profit annually (Bergman and Logan 2020).

College sports have in effect become recruitment grounds for major professional leagues. This stems from some sports, football and basketball in particular, having no minor league system in which aspiring professionals could learn their trade. By default, colleges are the only place where adequate coaching can be found, and recruitment has been geared to the college draft.

Yet colleges often claim that their sports departments operate close to the breakeven point, sometimes on the wrong side of it. Several factors help explain this seemingly contradictory situation. First, it is only the major televised sports that bring in the money, which is often used to subsidise other sporting activities. Second, the revenues are concentrated in a minority of colleges with just 69 of them responsible for more than half of the total generated. Third, the actual college accounts are somewhat creative with notional in-house transactions covering athletic scholarships, stadium depreciation, and other infrastructure costs.

Essentially, the colleges spend all the surpluses, which enables them to plead that they lose money on the operations of their athletic departments. They do not spend in a price auction for the services of the student-athlete, as National Collegiate Athletic Association (NCAA) regulations limit the financial compensation that an athlete can receive. Despite being the drawing cards for spectators and television audiences, the athletes receive little direct financial reward. Until 2014, no allowances at all were provided for living expenses: all the athletes obtained were fee scholarships, training, and the lure of future major league contracts. This changed after a report in 2013 by the National College Players Association showed that 86% of full scholarship football players lived below the poverty line: this despite often being committed to training and playing for over 40 hours a week. To maintain their 'amateur' status, they can receive financial aid above basic scholarships up to the federally defined full cost of attendance, plus a smattering of smaller benefits. Instead of payments to the student-athletes, there is an investment in quality coaches, facilities, and programmes from which the athlete can benefit. The NCAA has argued that price competition would be prohibitively expensive but has set no limits to the costs of non-price competition (Hoffer et al. 2015). Historically, there have always been systematic illegal payments, though nowhere near the level of the *economic rent* (see Chapter 5) that the student-athlete generates for the institution (Sack 1991). As yet, such transactions have been insufficient to create a free market for these talented athletes. Some states are now legislating for them to be able to endorse products and employ agents, and it is now being argued that the NCAA's bylaws which restrict any type of compensation – including direct payment for athletic accomplishments – might no longer hold up well in future antitrust challenges and that the NCAA's business model would be illegal in almost any other industry. Eventually, the lid will blow off the volcano, and the college athletes will be recognised for what they are: skilled professionals worthy of reward. However, there are others who do very well financially out of college sport. The head coaches of the four football teams who opened the 2019 season in a double-header took home a combined $26.4 million in total pay the previous season, and the coach of the University of Alabama football team was the highest-paid public employee in the state that year with earnings of

$8.3 million. Gus Malzahn lost his job at Auburn after eight years and was compensated with a buy-out of his remaining four years for $21.45 million.

Whether or not the surpluses are productively used, they still have to be generated. Two things should be born in mind. The first is that college sport television revenues are shared between all the colleges in the particular conference. However, colleges get to retain the money obtained from regular-season home gates, other venue revenue, sports apparel sponsorship, and, of course, alumni donations. These all increase when a team is a winning one, particularly if they make a championship final, thus driving the colleges into a sporting arms race in which, between 2006 and 2011, 207 NCAA Division I colleges increased their spending between 3% and 6% annually (Hoffer et al. 2015). College sports programmes have to replenish talent on an annual basis. Recruitment to a top football programme can cost close to a million dollars a year (Bergman and Logan 2016). The quality of athlete recruitment can assist in revenue raising. Bergman and Logan (2020) use nationwide high school player rankings in football to estimate that the recruitment of a five-star player raised college revenues by $650,000 annually; four-star players brought in $350,000, and three-star recruits were worth $150,000. Their work built on a previous study for basketball which showed that five-star recruits generated $600,000 and four-star ones $150,000.

Yet athletic departments continue to draw on allocated university funds (including from student fees) to supplement money generated by the sports themselves. Jewell (2020) found that the average generated revenues of major football colleges increased negatively (not really an oxymoron) from − $5.9 million in 2004 to − $14.4 million in 2016, an almost threefold increase in net losses.

Whether college sports generate sufficient funds to justify the spending on them rather than on more educationally relevant items remains an open question, given the difficulties in unravelling the intricacies of published accounts. The argument forwarded by advocates of spending on university sport is that a high-quality athletic team creates a positive spillover for the college's academic mission in attracting students with higher SAT scores. Research into this has produced mixed results. Using data covering 1993–2002 for 78 big-time sports universities, Tucker and Amato (2006) concluded that for basketball, there was no such 'advertising effect', though Tucker's (2005) work on the same institutions suggests a positive effect after the formation of the Bowl Championship Series in 1998, which created five bowl games for the top ten ranked colleges in football. Pope and Pope (2014), using a national data set that indicates where students choose to send their SAT scores, find that college sports success has a large impact on student applications. A school that has a stellar year in basketball or football receives up to 10% more SAT scores. This must relate to an awareness effect, as sports success does not necessarily relate to the quality or cost of the academic education that a university provides: would that the appointment of a star professor gain the same media attention!

Much more a proponent of genuine amateurism than the NCAA is the Gaelic Athletic Association, which runs Gaelic football and hurling across Ireland. It is a corporate organisation which, in 2017, earned €55.7 million from gate-money, sponsorship, and broadcasting contracts. Yet the sports it controls remain entirely amateur, as they have been since its foundation in 1884, and none of this income is spent on player wages. Uniquely in the elite sports world, the vast majority of its revenue (over 80% in 2017) is ploughed back into the grassroots of the sport, making Gaelic sports clubs the best-facilitated, mass sporting communities in Europe (Cronin 2020).

References

Andreff, Wladimir (2006), 'Voluntary Work in Sport' in Wladimir Andreff and Stefan Szymanski (eds.), *Handbook on the Economics of Sport* (Edward Elgar: Cheltenham), 219–224.

Bergman, Stephen and Trevon D. Logan (2016), 'The Effect of Recruit Quality on College Football Performance', *Journal of Sports Economics* 17.6, 578–600.

Bergman, Stephen and Trevon D. Logan (2020), 'Revenue per Quality of College Football Recruit', *Journal of Sports Economics* 21.6, 571–592.

Buchanan, James M. (1965), 'An Economic Theory of Clubs', *Economica* 32, 1–14.

Chudacoff, Howard P. (2015), *Changing the Playbook: How Power, Profit and Politics Transformed College Sports* (University of Illinois Press: Chicago).

Cronin, Mike (2020), 'Entrepreneurship in an Amateur World: The Gaelic Athletic Association in Ireland' in Dilwyn Porter and Wray Vamplew (eds.), *Sport and Entrepreneurship* (Routledge: Abingdon), 72–86.

Gregory, Sean (2017), 'Kids Sport Inc.', *Time*, 4 September 2017, 32–41.

Hoffer, Adam, Brad R. Humphreys, Donald J. Lacombe and Jane E. Ruseski (2015), 'Trends in NCAA Athletic Spending: Arms Race or Rising Tide?', *Journal of Sports Economics* 16.6, 576–596.

Jewell, R. Todd (2020), 'NCAA Expenditure and Efficiency: Analyzing Generated and Allocated Revenue in the Football Bowl Subdivision', *Journal of Sports Economics* 21.4, 363–390.

Pope, Devin G. and Jaren C. Pope (2014), 'Understanding College Application Decisions: Why College Sports Success Matters', *Journal of Sports Economics* 15.2, 107–131.

Porter, Dilwyn and Wray Vamplew (2018) 'Entrepreneurship, Sport, and History: An Overview', *The International Journal of the History of Sport* 35.7–8, 626–640.

Sack, Allen L. (1991), 'The Underground Economy of College Football', *Sociology of Sport Journal* 8, 1–15.

Szymanski, Stefan (2010), 'Economists and Sports History', *Journal of Sports History* 37.1, 72–81.

Tucker, Irvin B. (2005), 'Big-Time Pigskin Success: Is There an Advertising Effect?', *Journal of Sports Economics* 6.2, 222–229.

Tucker, Irvin B. and L. Ted Amato (2006), 'A Reinvestigation of the Relationship between Big-Time Basketball Success and Average SAT Scores', *Journal of Sports Economics* 7.4, 428–440.

Vamplew, Wray (2013), 'Theories and Typologies: A Historical Exploration of the Sports Club in Britain', *International Journal of the History of Sport* 30.14, 1569–1585.

5

PROFESSIONAL RECRUITMENT, EARNINGS, AND LABOUR RELATIONS

Professional Sportspeople

Professional sportspeople are different. They are different from other sports participants, as they are usually more talented, more skilled, bigger, and faster (or any combination of these depending on the sport). They are also different from normal workers with career structures and working lives at variance to those of most of the population. They retire earlier, face greater public appraisal of their work performance, have more erratic income flows, and often have to change their place of work on a regular basis. Moreover, many of them do not have similar employment rights to most other occupations. The professional team sportsperson does not have the freedom to give notice, quit their employment, and choose a fresh employer unless compensation is paid to their existing employer (who must be willing to accept the arrangement). Moreover, their employer can trade them to another employer either for cash or another player, a rarity in conventional labour markets.

For many sports enthusiasts, being paid to play sport is a childhood dream, but the reality is that players do not play sport; they work at it. Moreover, as on turtle beaches, many hatch but few make it to the sea. Consider the NBA, where, each year, perhaps 30 new names are added to the playing roster: this from some 10,000 basketballers who played in their high school year. Such a wastage rate has *economic welfare* implications, though Rosen and Sanderson (2001) point out that potential professional basketballers receive continuous feedback and can reassess their chances of making it at several stages. This reduces the *opportunity cost* (the next best economic use of their time) and they 'waste' less time pursuing a dream.

DOI: 10.4324/9781003128632-5

Recruitment

Professional sports clubs rely heavily on their *human capital* (players) to achieve results and/or profits. Unlike in most occupations, past performances in the sports industry are publicly documented, so employers know a good deal about potential recruits to their teams. In Britain and Europe, elite team recruitment tends to be between individuals and the relevant club, but in North America and Australia, there are two other major ways: zoning and the draft system, both of which deny players the right to negotiate with their preferred employer. In the former, traditional to Australia, players are allocated to teams via geographical location with variations based on birth, residence, and family ties. Technically, this should be random in aiding clubs, though, as Dabscheck (2004) comments, 'it is difficult to draw lines on maps to create areas capable of producing players of equal ability for all teams'.

More common, and thought more likely to reduce inequality between teams, is the player draft, usually incorporating some form of reverse order so that last year's wooden spoonist gets first choice of next year's recruits (in North America usually from the college system) and the reigning champion the last pick in each round. It seems straightforward, but there can be significant variations, including whether prior to the draft clubs can trade (either for money or players) their assigned draft position for a particular round, whether immediately after the draft clubs can trade players they have just drafted, whether extra (priority) choices are given to clubs with sustained poor performances over several seasons or an especially poor performance in any season, and whether other criteria are also used for the allocation of players, such as residence or kinship (Borland 2006). Moreover, if (say) there were ten teams and six rounds of picks, then the team with first choice only gains a real advantage over the premiers with its first pick over the latter's 60th, assuming that there is not much quality difference between the 11th and 10th picks, 21st and 20th, etc. Additionally, economic analysis has shown that the trading associated with draft choices can be problematic. It has been calculated that retrading in the NFL between 1998 and 2004 systematically overestimated the surplus value that could be derived from high draft selections or, in lay language, too high a price was paid for players and too high a salary was paid to those players (Borland 2006). It should be noted that the rules set a maximum salary level for each pick so that there is no salary battle between clubs.

In North America, MLB, far more than any other sport, also drafts straight from high school. The choice facing the aspiring professional is to accept an offer with the option of going to college later in life (though with an awareness that ex-professionals are prohibited from playing college sport) or going to college, gaining an education, and hoping that he will be drafted from college. The choice was not made any easier by the increased money within baseball, which led to a reversal of a decline in signing bonuses. In 2003, the average first-round signing bonus for a high school draftee was $1,877,000, a large sum to turn down when a career might be cut short by injury (Winfree and Molitor 2007). More recent work on the baseball draft has looked at the opportunity costs involved by the roughly 1,200 high school and college players signed each year. The vast majority would never play a major league season but spend time playing in the minors for less than $10,000 a season before they accepted that they were not going to progress. The conclusion of Pifer et al. (2020) was that, for those outside the upper quartile of picks, being drafted was not worth it economically.

Turning to an individual sport, a feature of the major golf tours is the restricted number of professionals who are allowed to compete on a regular basis by virtue of holding their 'card': all others are dependent on invitations and sponsors' picks. On the US PGA circuit, only the top 125 golfers on the money list at the end of the season retain their cards. Those that fall out, along with aspirants to come onboard, can attend the Qualifying School, a tough stroke-play competition over ten rounds with 25 tour spots available. Otherwise, they can downgrade to the National Tour, where a top-five finish in its money list will restore their card. The prize money on the National Tour is much less than on the PGA full tour, and there are fewer endorsement opportunities, as tournaments are not televised.

Mobility

Unlike most workers, professional sportspersons do not have the right to change their employers if they are offered a better deal somewhere else. Indeed, historically, once players had been signed by a particular club, that club held their property rights, and the players, unlike most workers, could not opt to change employer, even when their contract period was ended. For many years, FIFA operated a global employment system in which a soccer player could not transfer to another club without the permission of their former club. In the same vein in North America, most sports leagues had a reserve clause which restricted a player's ability to change clubs.

However, the past few decades have seen the eroding of such strict limitations on a player's mobility. In Europe, the Bosman ruling has allowed players to move once their contracts have expired and without the payment of any transfer fee; and in the United States, legal decisions have brought limited free agency after between three and seven years (depending on the sport), which has allowed players to sell their services in an open market.

When attempting to buy a player's contract from their existing club, the buying and selling clubs communicate with each other and negotiate a price: the player is rarely offered at a fixed price. The recruitment of free agents, however, is more of an auction with several clubs often interested in the player concerned. Each potential buyer will have their own valuation of the player based on past performance and estimated future potential. Making these ex ante (economist speak for before the event while *ex post* is after) valuations is not an exact science (even with sabermetrics) and future performances are not perfectly predictable. Someone is likely to make an error of judgement and overbid. Hence free agents (especially those with good agents) can expect to get a better deal than with their old clubs (who may be able to make a better judgement on the basis of their knowledge of the player, information not fully available to the other clubs). So when fans claim that a player is over-rated and overpaid, they may well be right (Cassing and Douglas 1980).

If clubs no longer had to pay compensation to the players' former clubs, then there was 'spare' money in the system. Enter agents to take advantage of the situation to make deals for their clients. Despite the frequent interventions by both governments and sports authorities into the operation of the sports labour market, much to the chagrin of many fans, the issue of sports agents has been left alone. Agents are intermediaries in the market between employers and professionals, who are regarded by many as bloodsuckers, draining money from sport and tempting their clients to switch allegiances too readily. They exist because knowledge in the professional sport labour market is not shared equally between negotiators, a case of what economists label *information asymmetry*. In the past, players (whose skills were in sport, not economics) were often at a disadvantage when negotiating their contracts, as they did not know their true market value, whereas agents have better awareness of what price the market might bear. The public might have a poor image of agents but not their clients.

Unlike most assets owned by sports companies which depreciate with use, players actually increase in value (at least for a while) as experience improves their on-field abilities as does *human capital formation* via coaching, skill development, and physical training. Who pays for this varies. The draft system in the United States passes on the costs of initial training to the colleges that participate in the NCAA structure. Apprenticeships in horse racing are a classic example of general on-the-job training in which employers attempt to cover the costs of education provision through low wages and long hours on the part of the trainee, with them often performing much of the manual labour that keeps the stable in operation. The ease with which players can change clubs has implications for the financing of human capital formation, as most of it is not club-specific in the benefits produced. If a club owns the property rights to their players, then it won't mind paying for their development (as it could either prevent players from leaving and taking the benefits of its expenditure with them or receive compensation within the transfer fee paid by the club to whom the player went). However, with the coming of free agency, the nature of the relationship changed, and clubs became less willing to incur human capital formation costs, some of which now had to be borne by the players: this, of course, has always been the case in non-team sports like golf and tennis.

Earnings

Earnings in most occupations are determined by a combination of the demand for labour of a certain type or quality, the available supply of such labour, and the productivity of that labour when at work. Sport generally follows that pattern but with some differences, especially where team sports are concerned.

Payment by results dominates individual sports remuneration. Prize money is a merit-based form of reward with larger sums paid the further a player progresses in a tennis tournament or the higher up the scoreboard in golf. Unlike many professional sports, tennis players and golfers essentially operate as independent contractors. There is no bargained minimum wage and no one to pick up the critical expenses required for day-to-day survival. They earn money from tournaments, playing exhibition matches, and signing endorsement deals, though it should be noted that at the lower end of the pyramid, many professionals make their living from coaching. The sad fact is that most tournament players make less than these teaching pros. In both golf and tennis, rankings are a key factor, as a player's position determines whether they will get an invitation to a particular tournament which, in a vicious circle of exclusivity, provides them with the opportunity to earn ranking points. Even if they make the tour, there are no guaranteed paydays for golfers. If you fail to make the cut (roughly the top 70 players after two of the four scheduled rounds) you earn nothing and still have to pay your travel and hotel expenses, as well as caddy fees. Of the 250 players on the US PGA Tour, each year half of them will lose their playing privileges and be demoted to the second-tier tour where only the top-100 prize money winners earn enough prize money to cover their travel costs and tournament fees. Even lower down the golfing pyramid are a set of tours which finance prize money out of the players' entry fees rather than sponsors' cash (Pastoriza et al. 2021). The skills required to make money can change. Putting ability has always been key to making money in golf, but Baugher et al. (2016), by assessing the earnings of all professionals on the American PGA Tour between 2006 and 2013 against standard performance statistics for various skills as collated by the tour, argue that since 2011, driving distance has become a more important factor. The likely reasons for this shift are the lengthening of courses allied with the narrowing of fairways and shortening of the rough. Nevertheless, even the best golfers still use their putter more than their driver, so putting remains a vital aspect of the professional game.

Jockeys fill an intermediate position between individual and team professionals. In horse racing, the quality of the horse is beyond the influence of the rider, but it is the jockey who can give the animal a chance of winning or eliminate that opportunity altogether. The vast majority of jockeys race on standard contract terms which provide for a guaranteed riding fee and a percentage of the prize money won. It is very much a *payment-by-results* system with an element of *non-risk payment* so that the jockey is not bearing all the risk of failure. A study of 413 flat-race jockeys riding in the United Kingdom between 1988 and 1995 showed that, with due allowance for the quality of the mount (as determined by racing analysts), the better riders still earned more money (Fernie and Metcalf 1999). Moreover, a comparison of outstanding riders, who, over time, had had retainers and also had ridden as freelance, showed that those on long-term retainer contracts to particular owners underperformed compared to those jockeys paid as freelancers. However, in arguing that incentive contracts generate superior performance to non-contingent payment systems, the authors failed to note a welfare aspect of the incentive system in that the basic riding fee leaves the vast majority of jockeys struggling to make a living, and indeed, they obtain more money from riding horses in training than on the racetrack. The authors noted the restricted supply side in the jockey market caused by requirements for low weight, an apprenticeship, and a licence but failed to point out that for every race, there are potentially 20 times more riders than rides available (Vamplew 2016).

There is prize money in team sports – though most of it goes to the club, not the players – but payment by results is not so applicable to team sports, as the effects of one player may be offset or enhanced by the performances of others on the team. Even with the growth of sporting metrics, it is not easy to gauge the effort, quality, commitment, and contribution of players. Hence generally players are paid by the season with some bonuses for achieving team targets. But why do some teams pay their players more, and why do stars get paid the most?

What has to be done is put a value on the team output so that wages can be based on it. This is where crowd figures or, more precisely, stadium revenue come into the equation (oops, I promised not to mention these). Economists will talk of *marginal revenue product* – the extra revenue created due to an addition of one unit of resource – but in reality, this is not easy to measure. Far simpler, but not simple, is to measure the contribution of team members to the playing performance of the side which is deemed to be the major attraction for fans, though astute readers will note that this seems to run contrary to the uncertainty of outcome hypothesis. Player productivity can be calculated in a two-stage process. First, is the contribution of a player to team performance, and then there is the contribution of that team performance to revenue accumulation by the club. This is easier said than done as, for example, the value of a win is not the same for all clubs, and *marginal revenue product* can be affected if stadium capacity is increased or a new television contract signed.

Sportspersons get their incomes from their ability to attract spectators and viewers. In individual sports, their income often comes in the guise of prize money, financed by gate-money revenue and television contracts. But not always. In one-off, head-to-head contests such as boxing, earnings are dictated by the fight contract by which the promoter negotiates a share of the gate depending on the relative strengths, reputations, and drawing power of the opponents. The nature of contracting in team sports is more complicated because contracts last longer than one match, though, like those in boxing, they are mainly determined by past performances. Stars get more because they attract more spectators. Sports teams make their money by selling a large volume at a small price (though some incredulous fans might debate what is 'small'), taking advantage of sport's ability for a few suppliers to fulfil the entire demand of many consumers, all of which can observe an event simultaneously. Star players might only be worth a few pounds more per spectator than journeyman professionals in the same team, but multiply that by the thousands who pay to watch at the game and on television, then the sky's the limit for their aggregate salaries.

An interesting question is whether you would pay more to a player who performs at a consistent level or one whose performance can fluctuate? A detailed study of 845 players in 3060 matches in the Bundesliga between 2005/2006 and 2009/2010 (34,413 observations) found strong evidence of a salary premium for talented players who perform inconsistently (based on player evaluations in *Kicker Sportmagazin*, a respected soccer magazine; Deutscher and Büschemann 2016). The reasoning behind this was that on their good days, such players can score the wonder goal or brilliant stopping tackle that determines the result in soccer, which is generally a low-scoring game, and that on their bad days, the rules allow them to be substituted.

In a conventional business, wages should not exceed the *marginal revenue product* (MRP) of the worker, as this would mean the firm was losing money on that worker's employment. Yet it is sometimes argued that utility-maximising sports firms overpay for their talent. Some fans express similar views when an expensive striker misses an open goal! On the other side of the pendulum, if workers are not paid their MRP, then the business is accruing *economic rent* from the transaction. Let me give a historical example of player exploitation. Australian cricketer, Donald Bradman, was the finest batsman of his era, and when he played in domestic test matches against England, attendance would be raised by some 7,000 spectators on the days that he was batting. Over his career, this amounted to extra gate revenue of at least A$65,000 (around A$3 million in 2020 prices), but he himself gained no benefit for this, as all the money accrued to the Australian Cricket Board. The Australian players were on similar salaries with nothing extra given to the star player, even though it was his aura and ability that brought in extra revenue. As the Australian Cricket Board was the sole employer for test matches, Bradman could not sell his talents elsewhere (Blackham and Chapman 2004). His only earnings alternative was to continue with his work in a stockbroker's office in Adelaide (cricket or stockbroking: quite a dilemma!). Whatever the Board offered to players was a 'take it or leave it' decision. This negotiating power enabled the Board to claim all the extra revenue generated by its star player. The discrepancy between what Bradman brought in for the Board and what he received in payment is labelled economic rent, the extra amount that he would have received in a freely operating market. If only he had had an agent! What agents have done is shift the distribution of *economic rent* away from the owners towards the players. In simple terms, economic rent is the extra income gained above a minimum level sufficient to persuade a worker to supply labour. This level is usually referred to as *transfer earnings* (not to be confused with transfer fees for players). Simmons (2007) believes that most of what he calls 'ordinary' players are underpaid relative to the revenues which they generate but also emphasises that they earn well above what they might receive in alternate employment, the opportunity cost of making a career in sport. Professional sportspersons get paid more than factory workers because there are relatively few substitutes for their services. Stars get paid most because they have even more of a scarcity value (Rosen and Sanderson 2001).

Finally, let's note that salaries and prize money are not the sole sources of income for professionals and indeed for star players can represent only a fraction of what they earn from endorsements and intellectual property rights. Prior to his transfer to Manchester United, Christiano Ronaldo, the star Portuguese footballer (though he only plays there in internationals), earned £365,000 a week from his club but obtained a further £73 million annually from other sources wishing to exploit his celebrity status. Every time he posts an endorsement on Instagram (on which he has over 200 million followers), he earns $1.6 million, bringing him $75.8 million annually. None of this is new, only the numbers have got bigger and the medium of technology has changed. The PGA Tour now allocates $40 million for distribution between the ten players who generate the most interest in the sport. Metrics used to assess this include the value of their social media and the number of internet searches they stimulate. What would Bobby Jones have said!

Contracts

Contracts have two major aspects: the pay structure and length of tenure, both of which have relevance for incentivisation of effort. Those for the NFL are typically for four years and have a tripartite pay structure. There is a basic salary (subject to an experience-determined minimum), but critically, and unlike in European football, this aspect of the salary is not guaranteed if the player is cut from the team. Second is a signing bonus, often a large sum, which can be paid at any time during the contract, though usually payment is staged over the term of the contract. Third, there are performance-related payments consisting of a team bonus (usually small) and personal bonuses based on targets achieved. In European football, contracts are generally for three years and cover a signing bonus (which can be deferred to the end of the contract), a regular salary, and bonus payments (usually at team level) for winning particular matches, reaching pan-European competitions, and securing trophies. One significant difference with the NFL is the use of contingency clauses which can reduce a salary if the team is relegated or increase the payment after a specified number of appearances (Simmons 2007). Economic studies of the effects of these contracts show that, in the Bundesliga, the teams that have higher proportions of performance-related pay in their salary structures tend to finish higher in the league (Frick 2007). In the NFL, it is higher team payroll that appears to result in better team performances (Simmons and Forrest 2004).

Simply recruiting the best players cannot guarantee success. The club must find ways of motivating its players and ensuring that they perform as well as they can. This is especially true where outcomes are not fully under the control of the athlete (as in most team sports). In such circumstances, not all of the pay can be outcome-related, and some payment insurance must be provided so that the athlete will accept part of the risk of failure. On the other hand (a favourite phrase of two-armed economists), contracts with no incentives or proportionally low to basic salaries run into the problem of what economists term *moral hazards*, where individuals have incentives to alter their behaviour because the risk is borne by others. In such circumstances, shirking becomes a possibility, not so much in the sense of players deliberately losing but that, at times during the season, they will underperform perhaps because of inadequate preparation for a game, lack of self-discipline with diet and recreational behaviour, or even declaring themselves unfit to play. There is a divergence between the interests of the principal (e.g. a club owner) and what economists term 'the agent' (in this case the player himself, not his agent): the player still gets paid despite not putting in full effort, but the team might lose the game.

Long-term contracts can benefit both players and their clubs. It gives the player security and locks in future costs for the clubs, as well as reduces their *transaction costs* (financial, time, and inconvenience) from continually having to renegotiate with their players. However, such contracts are, of course, written with incomplete knowledge of the future, and in practice, clubs generally have overpaid for the revenue-generating performances they received. Solow and Krautmann (2020) estimated that 89% of the 152 long-term MLB contracts operative in 2010 yielded negative returns with an average loss of $4.1 million per season, though there may have been some offsetting earnings from fan appeal via merchandising and broadcasting.

The length of a contract has often been thought to influence player behaviour. Clubs have to strike a balance between players feeling too secure in their jobs to perform up to expectations or so insecure that they are constantly looking to change clubs or are too anxious about the future to play well consistently. This may vary with the sport, so let's look at baseball, basketball, and soccer. A study of 108 free agents in MLB who signed new contracts before the beginning of the 2005 and 2006 seasons revealed that those who obtained multi-year ones generally created less value (calculated by translating player performance into contribution to team revenues) than they were expected to (Krautmann and Donley 2009). This fits with Marburger's (2003) study to test whether the abolition of reserve clauses in contracts (in which property rights reside with the employers) to free agency contracts (in which players can, in effect, sell themselves) would lessen shirking. He found that free agents with one- or two-year contracts outperformed comparable reserve-era players, but those with longer contracts did not. Turning to basketball, a study of 515 players in the NBA in the three years from 2000 noted that, as conventionally defined by basketball pundits (scores, rebounds, blocks, etc.), player productivity fell by 2%–4% when they were awarded a contract of more than two years (Berri and Krautmann 2006). In contrast, a study of 2,972 soccer players in the Bundesliga from 2002/2003 to 2012/2013 found that those with longer contracts performed more consistently, though this used partly subjective measures of performance from journalists (Buraimo et al. 2015). A major reason for this revolves around the long-term rolling contract which has developed in European football since the Bosman ruling (which allowed for free movement of labour). Under this, a player signs for up to perhaps five years but expects to enter fresh negotiations for an extension two or more years before the contract ends. This gave players an incentive to play well to secure a renewal. Single-year contracts might stimulate players to perform in the hope of a fresh offer, but the club runs the risk of losing the bulk of the team to better offers without any transfer payment compensation.

Retirement

Insecurity is the hallmark of a career in professional sport. It stems from many sources, including fear of injury, loss of form, threats to jobs from newcomers, and the inevitable short shelf-life of professional sportsmen. Every day the professional faces the possibility of no work tomorrow: losing in a tight finish, dropping an important catch, or being injured in a tackle can all lead to non-selection. Yet sometimes the players themselves can make the decision to retire, an important economic one given that their sporting life is a limited one. In a contact sport, the issue is often one of prolonging their earning capacity at the risk of life-changing injury. Recent publicity on the long-term effects of concussions has led to a wave of retirements from the NFL, with these players taking a proactive decision. Nevertheless, laboratory experiments – admittedly with no real long-term consequence at stake – suggest that players with multi-year contracts are likely to see out their obligations before leaving the sport, thus risking injury, while those on single-year contracts might reconsider their situation annually (DeAngelis and Kip Vicusi 2020). The introduction of mandatory annual neuropsychological assessments in the NFL and the National Hockey League (NHL) may influence such decision taking.

Unionism and Collective Bargaining

The arena of professional sport is the ultimate meritocracy in which productivity is the sole determinant of earnings. Or that is how it would operate in a perfect sporting economic world. However, some factors have mitigated true productivity-based determination of pay of professional sportspeople. Prime among these is unionism. Paradoxically, sport is not an industry suited to unionism. The units of production are small and geographically dispersed, there is a high degree of labour turnover, and generally high levels of job satisfaction. Moreover, unlike a production line, it is full of competing individuals, some much more talented than others. The ultimate basis of sport is competition with winners and losers, and generally, this is borne out in the earnings of the players: the best earn more than the journeymen. Hence unions do not negotiate salaries for their members, leaving this to the players themselves who usually employ agents for the purpose. A major issue then is for a union to be able to promote a commonality of interest that would embrace both journeymen and stars, rookies and veterans, so what is bargained collectively are working conditions, pension benefits, insurance, grievance procedures, and, in North America, league-wide arrangements, such as minimum salaries, aggregate payrolls, and salary caps (Rosen and Sanderson 2001). Player associations have also taken over the organisation of events in some sports, as with the PGA and Association of Tennis Professionals (ATP) tours: it is notable that these organisations do not call themselves trade unions, but, in effect, that is what they are.

Several attempts had been made over the years to establish player associations, but most of them were short-lived and unsuccessful: the employers were too powerful. However, legal decisions on the restraint of trade began to move in the players' favour and incentivised leagues to negotiate collective deals with player associations to protect any revised rules from legal attack (Rosen and Sanderson 2001; Dabscheck 2004). In North America, clubs sustained restrictive agreements by writing them into the agreement in exchange for various concessions to the players (Szymanski 2004). In 1984, the NBA players association agreed to a league-wide payroll cap on team salaries in exchange for a guaranteed 53% of NBA designated gross revenues (Vrooman 2000). At times, gaining such agreements has necessitated lockouts and strikes: indeed, the NHL lost the full 2004/2005 season due to a lockout.

There is a contrast in the objectives of sports unions and conventional trade unions. The basic aim of many sports unions is to bring in the free market and eliminate employer imposed restrictions on mobility and earnings, which contrasts with ordinary trade unions, which generally seek to impose restrictions (their own) on the labour market to prevent exploitation by employers. That said, both sets of unions wish to become monopoly sellers of labour so as to squeeze as much from the employers as they can (Szymanski 2004).

References

Baugher, Carson D., Jonathan P. Day and Elvin W. Burford Jr. (2016), 'Drive for Show and Putt for Dough? Not Anymore', *Journal of Sports Economics* 17.2, 207–215.

Berri, David J. and Daniel R. Krautmann (2006), 'Shirking on the Court: Testing for the Incentive Effects of Guaranteed Pay', *Economic Inquiry* 44.4, 536–546.

Blackham, Julian and Bruce Chapman (2004), 'The Value of Don Bradman: Additional Revenue in Australian Ashes Tests', *Economic Papers* 23.4, 369–385.

Borland, Jeff (2006), 'Economic Design and Professional Sporting Competitions', *Australian Economic Review* 39.4, 435–441.

Buraimo, Babatunde, Bernd Frick, Michael Hickfang and Rob Simmons (2015), 'The Economics of Long-Term Contracts in the Footballers' Labour Market', *Scottish Journal of Political Economy* 62.1, 8–24.

Cassing, James and Richard W. Douglas (1980), 'Implications of the Auction Mechanism in Baseball's Free Agent Draft', *Southern Economic Journal* 47.1, 110–121.

Dabscheck, Braham (2004), 'The Imperfect Market for Players', *Economic Papers* 23.4, 345–354.

DeAngelis, Scott and W. Kip Vicusi (2020), 'When to Walk Away and When to Risk It All', *Journal of Sports Economics* 21.5, 525–547.

Deutscher, Christian and Arne Büschemann (2016), 'Does Performance Consistency Pay off Financially for Players? Evidence From the Bundesliga', *Journal of Sports Economics* 17.1, 27–43.

Fernie, Sue and David Metcalf (1999), 'It's Not What You Pay It's the Way That You Pay It and That's What Gets Results: Jockeys' Pay and Performance', *Labour* 13.2, 385–411.

Frick, Bernd (2007), 'The Football Players' Labour Market: Empirical Evidence from the Major European Leagues', *Scottish Journal of Political Economy* 54.3, 422–446.

Krautmann, Anthony C. and Thomas D. Donley (2009), 'Shirking in Major League Baseball Revisited', *Journal of Sports Economics* 10.3, 292–304.

Marburger, Daniel R. (2003), 'Does the Assignment of Property Rights Encourage or Discourage Shirking? Evidence from Major League Baseball', *Journal of Sports Economics* 4.1, 19–34.

Pastoriza, David, Jean-François Plante and Nadjib Lakhlef (2021), 'Are Foreigners at a Disadvantage in a Global Labor Market?', *Journal of Sports Economics* 22.6, 615–638.

Pifer, N. David, Christopher M. McLeod, William J. Travis and Colten R. Castleberry (2020), 'Who Should Sign a Baseball Contract? Quantifying the Financial Opportunity Costs of Major League Draftees', *Journal of Sport Economics* 21.7, 746–780.

Rosen, Sherwin and Allen Sanderson (2001), 'Labour Markets in Professional Sports', *Economic Journal* 111, F47–F68.

Simmons, Rob (2007), 'Overpaid Athletes? Comparing American and European Football', *WorkingUSA* 10.4, 457–471.

Simmons, Rob and David Forrest (2004), 'Buying Success: Relationships Between Team Performance and Wage Bills in the US and European Sports Leagues' in Rodney Fort and John Fizel (eds.), *International Sports Economics Comparisons'* (Praeger: Westport, CT), 123–140.

Solow, John L. and Anthony C. Krautmann (2020), 'Do You Get What You Pay For? Salary and Ex-Ante Player Value in Major League Baseball', *Journal of Sports Economics* 21.7, 705–722

Szymanski, Stefan (2004), 'Is There a European Model of Sports?' in Rodney Fort and John Fizel (eds.), *International Sports Economics Comparisons'* (Praeger: Westport, CT), 19–38.

Vamplew, Wray (2016), ' Still Crazy After All Those Years: Continuity in a Changing Labour Market for Professional Jockeys' in Wray Vamplew (ed.), *Numbers and Narratives: Sport, History and Economics* (Routledge: Abingdon), 84–105.

Vrooman, John (2000), 'The Economics of American Sports Leagues', *Scottish Journal of Political Economy* 47.4, 364–398.

Winfree, Jason A. and Christopher J. Molitor (2007), 'The Value of College: Drafted High School Baseball Players', *Journal of Sports Economics* 8.4, 378–393.

6

SPORTSWOMEN AND GENDER ECONOMICS

Introduction

My initial intention was not to write a separate chapter on women in sport but to integrate them into the other chapters where appropriate. However, the publishers insisted. It was a prime example of market forces (no separate chapter, no contract!) but also of market incentives (separate chapter and we'll give you an expensive book on women in sport gratis): a no brainer. On reflection, I then began to realise that there were issues, and not just of discrimination, where economists might have something to say on the sporting experience of women: on women as sports fans and women as participants at both amateur and professional levels. I also became aware, as two sports economists pointed out in 2013, that there was a 'surprising dearth of interest among economists in women's sport' (Leeds and Leeds 2013). To their discredit, as will be apparent from this chapter, sports economists have done little to rectify this position in the past decade.

Women as Fans and Participants

In their survey of sport in the United States, Montgomery and Robinson (2013) show that basically the major influences on women becoming sports spectators are the same as for men: age, education, and income. Specifically, younger, more educated women with higher incomes are more likely to watch sport. However, they also argue that an increase in participation (though not, of course, to the level of men) has led to a concomitant rise in female attendance as spectators at sports events. They argue that this is because they have accumulated sports-related *human capital*, a knowledge and understanding of particular sports which enables them to appreciate what they see. Married women are more likely to attend sports events than single ones. According to Montgomery and Robinson (2010), this is not

DOI: 10.4324/9781003128632-6

because they have gained sports capital from their husbands but more likely due to individuals with similar amounts of sports capital being attracted to each other. I would raise two caveats and a suggestion. First, there was no clarification of whether sports events included those for children in which case soccer moms would certainly be in attendance. Second, the studies concentrated on physical spectatorship at sports events, whereas including televised sport might have different results. Third, that women possess sports capital might be of relevance to those marketing sport to women, particularly those who have tended not to treat them as knowledgeable about sport and failed to authentically communicate with them as serious sports fans (Brown and Nalani Butler 2019). Many leagues and teams miss or fail to meet the needs of an entire customer segment because they do not understand the communication and marketing preferences of their female fans (Esmonde et al. 2015).

In looking at sports participation in Australia, Booth and Leeds (2013) suggest that a useful model with which to examine women's (and men's) choice of sporting activity is that of allocating personal time by hypothesising that different leisure activities bring unique rewards. This allows us to analyse people's participation in sport, as engaging in sport is part of their broader *work/leisure trade-off*. Women have different preferences, which are reflected in the findings from the Australian Bureau of Statistics material that women undertake physical leisure activities for their health and well-being, while men participate for socialisation and competition. This model also has implications for spectatorship, as men can satisfy their desires for competition and social interaction by watching sport, but this would do little for women's fitness or weight loss.

Ross and Leeds did not consider discrimination as a possible influence on participation in particular sports, but certainly, it has worked that way in many countries. This is a cultural prejudice rather than an economic one, but economics can be used to mitigate it. In Scottish golf, a sport often claimed to be a democratic one open to all, several private clubs have been reluctant to allow women to join. A prime example was Muirfield Golf Club in Scotland, which since its foundation in 1744 had refused to admit women into membership. In 2016, a vote to allow female members failed to secure the two-thirds majority required. The Royal & Ancient Golf Club, the ruling body of British golf, immediately removed Muirfield from the roster of clubs deemed worthy to hold the Open Championship. A second vote in 2017 found over 80% in favour of women being admitted. Guess what? Muirfield is now back on the roster.

In the United States, government intervention has forced action on amateur sport in one area, that of the colleges. In 1964, the federal government passed civil rights legislation which prohibited discrimination on the basis of race, colour, religion, or national origin by employers who received federal funds. In 1972, Title IX was tagged onto this and addressed discrimination in education, including intercollegiate sport. A study by Averett and Estelle (2013) investigated whether post-secondary educational institutions had met the compliance standard of 'substantial proportionality' and showed that, although Title IX had increased female participation in sport, most institutions had not been compliant. One reason was that penalties for non-compliance had not been enforced. The other was budget constraints. There has been a reluctance to lessen men's sports by shifting budget provisions to female ones, so budget expansion has been the way forward. Stafford (2004) found that compliance was more likely in large institutions (more budget to play with) that had relatively few women (less expensive to comply) and no football programme (the largest call on the budget). Little had changed a decade later (Averett and Estelle 2013).

The impact of the demands of sports training on student-athletes' educational attainment has long been discussed. Here it can be suggested that female student-athletes perform better academically than their male counterparts. Fairweather (2013) analysed the graduation rates at institutions with top-level sports programmes. Individual student data was not accessible, so he had to work with subsets of data, though, unfortunately, not at the level of identifiable sports. Nevertheless, he was able to show that the average graduation rate for male athletes was three percentage points lower than for male non-athletes and 6.5% less than the overall graduation rate, while, female athletes had a rate 9% higher than other females and 11.5% higher than the overall rate.

Unequal Pay for (Un)equal Work?

In 2017, only two women featured in the rankings of Australia's top 50 sport earners: six-time world surfing champion Stephanie Gilmore, at number 39 with A$1.75 million and World Golf Hall-of-Famer Karrie Webb, creeping into last place with $1.28 million, though both falling far behind the top two men: basketballer Andrew Bogut who earned A$16.2 million just ahead of golfer Adam Scott with A$15.5 million (Sherry and Taylor 2019). Yet, also in Australia, the Victorian Open Golf Championships of 2019 in a co-sanctioned event of the Men's European PGA and the Ladies PGA Tours, were played on the same course (with length differences) on the same days for the same prize money. Such equal treatment is rare in professional sport, with tennis being the pioneer and main proponent. In 1973, the US Open became the first major tennis tournament to offer equal prize money. This success was tempered by the fact that it took another 28 years before another Grand Slam tournament, the Australian Open followed suit.

No one doubts that female professionals are generally paid less than male players, though it is hard to actually test for gender discrimination as men and women rarely compete against each other. One sport where they do is horse racing, and here Ray and Grimes (1993) found that in American racing, men had twice as many rides as women but secured nine times the level of prize money, raising strong suspicions of discrimination (in giving men the better horses to ride) by the owners and trainers who employ the jockeys.

At the professional level, discrimination can be economically rational. The theory of this will be discussed in a later chapter, but, put simply, it is a matter of the revenue that athletes bring in for their clubs or promoters. What is it worth to be world champions in soccer? Well, when the US women won the title in 2015, the team aggregated $2 million, which contrasts poorly with the men's team's $8 million reward at the FIFA World Cup of 2014 despite only reaching the last 16. This was a function of the prize money made available by FIFA, $15 million for the women's tournament and $576 million for the men's. In turn, this was influenced by the respective sponsorship for the two events of $17 million and $529 million (Leeds et al. 2018).

The problem is often put as a socio-cultural one of discrimination, one that brings the prejudice of amateur sport into the professional arena. However, it is essentially one of economics and revolves around what is meant by 'equal work'. Too much attention has been focused by the proponents of equality on the input aspect of the definition and insufficient on the output. At the elite level, successful sportswomen clearly put in as much effort as their male counterparts: in training hard, in developing skills, and in pushing themselves to the limit. However, economists would ask about the *marginal revenue product* of all this effort: more simply, how many spectators or television viewers does women's sport attract? If it can be demonstrated that the revenue raised by a female star is commensurate with that of a man, equal pay should follow (unless we then get back to social gender discrimination). Would the women pressing for equal pay in sport be prepared to give the same to junior and veteran athletes or elite disabled sportspersons? Unless sport becomes a social service, then it is the market that determines rewards. This basic economic principle explains why in men's sport, Premier League footballers earn more than field hockey players. Physical differences mean that men and women rarely compete together in a sport, but, if they did, then equality of reward should not be a problem, as the prize money would be gender-blind. All this means that if there is to be equality of rewards in women's and men's sports, there has to be a cross-subsidisation from the men's events to the women's. Commercial promoters do not see this as something they should take the responsibility for. However, as suggested next, it could be done by others.

The aforementioned *consumer sovereignty* argument does not disallow the fact that historic cultural discrimination has contributed to the downgrading of women's sport in the marketplace. Decades, centuries even, of denigrating women in sport, offering less and poorer quality media coverage (a vicious circle of under-demand here), and promoting it as a poor version of men's sport have strongly influenced spectator demand, the very thing that generates revenue for clubs. That said, governments could influence future demand levels by dedicating funds to women's sport and passing legislation (like Title IX but with more enforcement) to outlaw discrimination in amateur sport. In command economies, they could bypass the market and pay higher wages to professional sportswomen employed by the state or provincial governments. Sport governing bodies, responsible for selecting (and paying) international teams, could offer equal pay, as they have a proselytising mission beyond making money. Some already have. In 2017, the Norwegian Football Association was the first governing body to determine equal pay for female and male players on national teams. Equal pay was achieved because the male national team was willing to forgo a specific proportion of their revenues generated through commercial activities. The resulting pay differences tended to be minimal for males, though payments for females increased significantly (Wicker 2019). A similar situation occurred in ice hockey where the highly successful United States' women's team was eventually promised increased compensation and benefits similar to the men's programme. Again, it was at least partially made possible by financial support from the men's players, who, coming from the NHL, earned far more than the women who did not have professional league employment (Koller 2019). A final possibility would be financial benefactors willing to spend money to achieve titles, but they would have to consider what particular title was worth winning.

However, we are venturing into the territory of 'shoulds' and 'oughts'. As it stands, women's sport does not bring in enough money to justify equality of payment with men's sport. There are some relatively successful women's sports leagues, such as the Women's National Basketball Association (WNBA), but they do not, as yet, bring in sufficient revenue to allow for equality of earnings. However, as an economic historian, I suggest that a time dimension should be considered. If we look at the early histories of the NBA, MLB, and NFL, what do we find? Leagues struggling to keep teams afloat, to attract fans, and to find permanent homes for their clubs, a pattern matched by the WNBA. In 1969–1970, the average NBA team drew just 7,563 fans per game, a smaller crowd than an average WNBA team attracted after 21 seasons. Attendance today is 17,884 per game in the NBA, but 47 years ago, it was only 42.3% of this mark. Similarly, after 21 years, MLB average league attendance was only 7,391 per game. In other words, MLB, after 21 seasons, drew 49.3% of the fans it was drawing per game 47 years later. Attendance for MLB continued to grow after that. In 2017, the average team drew 30,042 fans. The NFL fared better, but still, average attendance in 1947 (30,624) was 48.9% of that in 1994 (Berri 2019). It is quite likely that crowds at WNBA games will increase substantially, and perhaps as events conspire to raise its profile, the time needed to double attendances will be telescoped compared to the experience of men's major league sports.

All this said, there is no doubt that in thoroughbred horse racing, the one major professional sport in which women and men directly compete, there is non-economic discrimination against women. In horse racing, it is not the size of the audience either at the racecourse or in front of the television screen that influences jockeys' earnings but where the riders finish in races. It is performance on the racetrack that affects the decision by owners and trainers as to whom to employ to ride their horses, and this is what determines their income. Jockeys are private contractors hired by owners and trainers to ride their horses for which they receive a fixed standard fee plus an institutionalised percentage of the prize money (10% for first, 5% for second and third). In the United States, women comprise about 12% of all jockeys but get only 6% or so of the rides and, on average, these mounts tend to be of lower-rated horses. Yet a study of nearly a million rides by over 2,000 jockeys between 2016 and 2018 showed that, other things being equal, the productivity – as measured by being in the money by finishing first, second, or third – was not significantly different between the genders (Binder et al. 2021). The model used was based on *probit* (short for probability units) analysis which isolated the effect of gender on riding success by making allowances for such variables as the quality of horse ridden, the type of track, and jockey weight allowances, and career length and argued that, *ceteris paribus* (economist speak for other things being equal), male jockeys would place in 39% of their rides and female riders 34%, with respective winning percentages of 13% and 11%. Horse owners, however, do not appreciate *ceteris paribus*. What they see is a horse (that probably had no chance anyway) with a female rider trailing behind the leaders, a view that reinforces the traditional prejudice that women do not have the physical strength to race against men. Although not assessed in as much detail as the US case, several studies show that discrimination against female jockeys is a worldwide phenomenon. Only in New Zealand do they get more opportunities, but that is because New Zealand racing is a secondary market, as the better male jockeys opt to cross the Tasman to ride in Australia where the potential rewards are greater.

As I completed this chapter, the English Cricket Board was launching its new competition, the Hundred. It has made a great play of gender parity, with the women's competition being publicised and televised as much as the men's. However, the salaries tell a different story. For men, they range between £24,000 and £100,000, but for women, they are between £3,600 and £15,000.

Are Female Sportspersons Different?

Turning away from discrimination to other matters. In several sports, allowance has been made for physical gender differences, such as lower nets in volleyball, fewer high hurdles in athletics, and lighter and smaller balls in both basketball and handball. There is no such differentiation in tennis where the net remains at three feet high whether it is men or women who are playing. This has consequences for the competitiveness of their respective matches. Based on an analysis of every set in 24 men's (3,844 sets) and 23 women's (3,034 sets) prestigious singles tournaments in 2010, Krumer et al. (2016) conclude that top-level men's tennis is more competitive than women's, as the average number of games in each set was higher, a result that held even after allowances for player rankings and court surfaces. This, they found, was almost entirely due to gender differences in height and body mass index, which meant that men were more likely to hold the more powerful serves. Ultimately, this could influence crowd attendance figures if the *competitive balance* hypothesis holds for tennis.

Leeds and Leeds (2013) used 11 major women's skating tournaments in 2009/2010 to assess whether women respond differently than men to economic incentives, a topic that has relevance away from sports. Experiments in controlled environments suggested that women perform worse in competitive situations than men, which has implications for female business executives and managers. In contrast, in the real world, albeit a sporting one, female figure skaters responded positively to incentives (where the reward was determined competitively, with the winner receiving a disproportionate share), were not averse to competition, were more resilient in the face of negative feedback (low scores in the short programme that precedes the longer freestyle one), and did not avoid competing with other elite skaters. This contrasts with the findings of a previous study on female golfers

(Matthews et al. 2007) which suggested that female golfers played worse in final rounds when higher prize money was on offer. One significant issue to my mind was that there was no prize money offered in several of the competitions in ice skating, just titles, though, of course, winning a European or world title can bring economic rewards through sponsorship. An examination by Anbarci et al. (2016) of 331 men's matches and 149 women's at the tier-one level in the ATP and Women's Tennis Association (WTA) tennis tours between 2006 and 2008 suggested no significant difference in line-call challenges between the genders, except when it came to tiebreaks. Then women were more reluctant to challenge (but were more successful when they did), whereas men challenged much more. The authors argue that this demonstrated a win-at-all-costs mentality by male players. I am less sure of this given the limited number of observations.

At a lower level of sport, purely amateur with only intrinsic incentives, Pikos and Straub (2020) examined nine-pin bowling in German mixed-gender leagues to assess if men and women compete in the same way. Following over 500,000 observations from around 11,000 games, they found that men tended to beat women, but this was due to the general ability of those players rather than being gender-related. Moreover, both genders reacted similarly to performing under pressure in tight situations. What must be stressed, however, is that this is a sport where competitors cannot significantly influence the play of an opponent, as they can in tennis.

Although a later chapter will examine the global migration of sportspersons, here let us look at a special case in women's sport, the influx of South Korean golfers into the Ladies PGA (LPGA) Tour, the pinnacle of female golf internationally. The move began in the late 1990s, and currently, there are some 70 Korean players with LGPA Tour cards. Migration theory suggests we need an assessment of the relative influence of 'pull' and 'push' factors to explain the influx. The obvious answer to why they have joined the tour is the prize money offered on their domestic tour compared with that of the LGPA, which, in 2004, was less than a tenth. The relative gap has narrowed, but the absolute one has widened so that in 2019, while the Korean Ladies Professional Golf Association (KLGPA) prize fund totalled $21.7 million, the LPGA players were competing for $70.6 million. However, the answer is less straightforward than might appear, as two other issues have to be considered: the distribution of that prize money and the relative quality of the golfers trying to win it. The LGPA money continued to be greater than that of the KLPGA much further down the tail, so a worse positional performance in America could still bring in more money. Moreover, world performance rankings for female golfers suggested that the Koreans could do well on the LGPA Tour, especially when putting rankings were considered (all golfers know the old adage that 'you drive for show, but putt for dough'). Hence the expected earnings for a Korean golfer on the PGA tour in 2001 was $375,000 compared to $34,000 if they stayed at home (Lee et al. 2013): no wonder they ventured overseas, especially when the estimated pecuniary costs of doing so equated with the earnings of the 90th ranked player on the tour, a position many of them anticipated exceeding. In contrast, few South Korean men have joined the PGA tour despite the relative levels of prize money being even more disparate. Most likely this resulted from differences in the intensity of competition on the men's tour, which made it much harder to achieve high placings consistently, plus the fact that it was also more difficult to secure a tour card for the PGA than the LPGA.

References

Anbarci, Nejat, Jungmin Lee and Aydogan Ulker (2016), 'Win at All Costs or Lose Gracefully in High-Stakes Competition? Gender Differences in Professional Tennis', *Journal of Sports Economics* 17.4, 323–353.

Averett, Susan L. and Sarah M. Estelle (2013), 'The Economics of Title IX Compliance in Intercollegiate Athletics' in Eva Marikova Leeds and Michael A. Leeds (eds.), *Handbook of the Economics of Women in Sports* (Edward Elgar: Cheltenham), 175–212.

Berri, David (2019), 'The Relative Success Story of the WNBA' in Nancy Lough and Andre N. Guerin (eds.), *Routledge Handbook of the Business of Women's Sport* (Routledge: Abingdon), 191–202.

Binder, Alexander D., Paul W. Grimes and Russell G. Winterbotham (2021), 'In the Money: Gender and Jockey Success on the Thoroughbred Racetrack', *Journal of Sports Economics* 22.3, 295–328.

Booth, Ross and Michael A. Leeds (2013), 'Participation in Women's Sport in Australia' in Eva Marikova Leeds and Michael A. Leeds (eds.), *Handbook of the Economics of Women in Sports* (Edward Elgar: Cheltenham), 40–55.

Brown, Brandon and B. Nalani Butler (2019), 'Examining Successful (and Non-Successful) Branding and Marketing Efforts' in Nancy Lough and Andre N. Guerin (eds.), *Routledge Handbook of the Business of Women's Sport* (Routledge: Abingdon), 367–378.

Esmonde, Katelyn, Cheryl Cooky and David Andrews (2015), '"It's Supposed to Be about the Love of the Game, not the Love of Aaron Rodgers' Eyes": Challenging the Exclusions of Women Sports Fans', *Sociology of Sport Journal* 32.1, 22–48.

Fairweather, B. Erin (2013), 'The Impact of Increased Academic Standards of Proposition 16 on the Graduation Rates of Women and Men in Division 1A Intercollegiate Athletics' in Eva Marikova Leeds and Michael A. Leeds (eds.), *Handbook of the Economics of Women in Sports* (Edward Elgar: Cheltenham), 233–248.

Koller, Dionne (2019), 'The New Gender Equity in Elite Women's Sports' in Nancy Lough and Andre N. Guerin (eds.), *Routledge Handbook of the Business of Women's Sport* (Routledge: Abingdon), 217–226.

Krumer, Alex, Mosi Rosenboim and Offer Moshe Shapir (2016), 'Gender. Competitiveness, and Physical Characteristics: Evidence From Professional Tennis', *Journal of Sports Economics* 17.3, 234–259.

Lee, Young Hoon, Ilhyeok Park, Joon-Ho Kang and Younghan Lee (2013), 'An Economic Analysis of the Sudden Influx of Korean Female Golfers into the LPGA' in Eva Marikova Leeds and Michael A. Leeds (eds.), *Handbook of the Economics of Women in Sports* (Edward Elgar: Cheltenham), 388–409.

Leeds, Eva Marikova and Michael A. Leeds (2013), 'Do Men and Women Respond Differently to Economic Contests? The Case of Men's and Ladies Figure Skating' in Eva Marikova Leeds and Michael A. Leeds (eds.), *Handbook of the Economics of Women in Sports* (Edward Elgar: Cheltenham), 319–344.

Leeds, Michael A., Peter Von Allmen and Victor A. Matheson (2018), *The Economics of Sports* (Routledge: Abingdon).

Matthews, Peter, Paul Sommers and Francisco Peschiera (2007), 'Incentives and Superstars on the LPGA Tour', *Applied Economics* 39, 87–94.

Montgomery, Sarah S. and Michael D. Robinson (2010), 'Empirical Evidence on the Effects of Marriage on Male and Female Attendance at Sports and Arts', *Social Science Quarterly* 91.1, 99–116.

Montgomery, Sarah S. and Michael D. Robinson (2013), 'Women's Attendance at Sports Events' in Eva Marikova Leeds and Michael A. Leeds (eds.), *Handbook of the Economics of Women in Sports* (Edward Elgar: Cheltenham), 21–39.

Pikos, Anna Katharina and Alexander Straub (2020), 'Mind the Absent Gap: Gender-Specific Behavior in Nonprofessional Sport', *Journal of Sports Economics* 21.3, 215–233.

Ray, Margaret A. and Paul W. Grimes (1993), 'Jockeying For Position: Winnings and Gender Discrimination on the Thoroughbred Racetrack', *Social Science Quarterly* 74.1, 46–61.

Sherry, Emma and Chelsey Taylor (2019), 'Professional Women's Sport in Australia' in Nancy Lough and Andre N. Guerin (eds.), *Routledge Handbook of the Business of Women's Sport* (Routledge: Abingdon), 123–133.

Stafford, Sarah H. (2004), 'Progress Towards Title IX Compliance: The Effect of Formal and Informal Enforcement Mechanisms', *Social Science Quarterly* 85.5, 1469–1486.

Wicker, Pamela (2019), ' Public Expenditure on Women's Sport and Gender Equality Among Recipients of Public Expenditure in European Sport' in Nancy Lough and Andre N. Guerin (eds.), *Routledge Handbook of the Business of Women's Sport* (Routledge: Abingdon), 204–216.

7

ATTENDANCES AND AUDIENCES

Attracting Paying Customers

Back in Chapter 1, it was noted that most sports economists believe that crowds will be larger the more equal the contest and the less predictable the result. This has led to actions by sports leagues and sports promoters to try and create more competitively balanced tournaments, often by interventions in the labour and product markets, such as revenue sharing and reverse-order draft arrangements for the recruitment of players. These will be discussed further in Chapter 9, and for the time being, we will look just at the competitive-balance hypothesis in a little more detail.

Many years ago, when I first ventured into sports economics, I was convinced by the logic of the uncertainty of outcome and competitive-balance hypotheses. Now I am less sure: there is no unambiguous evidence that competitive balance positively influences stadium attendance, nor, I should add, that it has no effect. For a resumé of research results, see Cox (2018). Of the more recent contributions to the literature, Gyimesi's (2020) study of league positional changes in 19 European football leagues between 10 and 48 seasons showed that a high degree of change over several seasons, especially regarding the top five positions, positively affects average stadium attendance per game (after allowing for any stadium expansion). Humphreys and Miceli (2019) note that leagues are not run by social planners keen to maximise the *economic welfare* of sports fans but by business interests more concerned with revenue streams, and suggest that both can be satisfied by the pursuit of the *uncertainty of outcome* in league fixtures. They focus on two propositions. The first is that all partisan fans want to see their teams win, an impossibility in practice, but creating uncertainty of outcome gives partisan fans the opportunity of their teams winning, which also satisfies the second proposition, that non-partisan fans would prefer a close encounter. In circumstances where the audience contains both partisan and non-partisan fans, uncertainty of outcome is the optimal position that

DOI: 10.4324/9781003128632-7

should maximise overall attendances and also economic welfare (a situation which cannot be improved by further aiding one group of fans).

One problem is that it is often inferred that competitive balance will ensure uncertainty of outcome, but Forrest and Simmons (2002) argue that this is not necessarily the case because of the phenomenon of home-ground advantage, well-known in many sports. In the case of the English Football League (EFL), where they examined 872 fixtures in the 1997–1998 season, roughly two-thirds were won by the home club. This led them to suggest that the most unpredictable fixtures would be weak home sides against stronger away teams, not something countenanced in the competitive-balance hypothesis. Their study went on to suggest that even uncertainty of outcome might not necessarily raise attendances. They compared actual attendances with the betting odds on the game set by specialist bookmakers. These were what are termed 'fixed odds', which do not vary with the amount of money risked by punters, so they can be viewed as reflecting the actual chances of each team as determined by experts. However, this study had to omit the EPL from its calculations, as stadiums were often filled to capacity, meaning that the actual level of unfulfilled demand could not be measured.

As for the EPL itself, using a variety of measures, all of them variants on analysing the dispersion of winning percentages, Lee and Fort (2012) have computed the degree of competitive balance in elite English football at the end of each season. Although their data ran from 1888, it ceased in 2007, but the results were unambiguous. Historically, the twenty-first century has exhibited the greatest imbalance, followed by the last decade of the twentieth century; in other words, the years of the EPL. Despite Leicester's surprise premiership in 2016, the two-and-a-half decades have generally been dominated by the 'Big Four' of Arsenal, Chelsea, Liverpool, and Manchester United, with the recent addition of Manchester City. Yet, crowds have not diminished. Given the constant rise in attendance, Szymanski (2010) has commented that 'contrary to received wisdom, the fans did not seem to care too much about competitive balance'. It may be that the quality of the product offered for sale, in particular the skills demonstrated by the players, has outweighed the uncertainty principle as a demand factor. Ultimately, an uncompetitive league might deter spectators from attending (apart from fans of the winning teams), but we do not know where the actual tipping point is.

The relative drawing power of teams is another factor that could offset the competitive balance in maximising attendance. Fans, home fans especially, want to see their teams win, so, if a consistently winning team has a larger spectator catchment area or a greater capacity stadium, then aggregate attendance (or, as economists would put it, total *welfare* in the form of *fan utility*) would be higher by not taking action to unduly undermine that team's performances by competitive-balance strategies. Moreover, if there is revenue sharing, this might also be in the interest of the less successful clubs. Let us imagine a football league with four teams from London (say) Arsenal, Chelsea, Spurs, and West Ham, and another four from the South Yorkshire ex-coalfields (say) Barnsley, Rotherham, Huddersfield, and Doncaster (I told you economic theory could make unrealistic assumptions). In whose financial and welfare (call this fan support) interests would it be to give all these teams equal chances to win that tournament? Berri et al. (2004) summarise the literature as suggesting that consumers prefer to see their (home) team win but do not want this to be absolutely certain.

A further major issue to be faced is that of actually measuring competitive balance. If you set achieving this as an objective, how do you know if you have attained it? There are as many ways to measure competitive balance as there are faults in my golf swing (this from someone with the maximum allowable handicap). Each sports economist who ventures into the area seems to have their own version. They can range from the extremely simple of counting how many titles a few of the clubs have won to multi-variate analysis, with the latter obviously full of equations (and we don't want to go there). An important point to make is that few, if any, of these studies are fully comparable. They deal with different sports in different cultures, with leagues and competitions that have different organisational and operational set-ups such as play-offs for the title rather than just the season-long performance, promotion, and relegation (sometimes with play-offs, sometimes not) and one-off tournaments with or without seedings of fancied players. Put simply, the winner of the Super Bowl has had a different journey to the team relegated from the lowest tier of the Scottish Football League and not just in terms of playing success. Any measure of competitive balance has to be appropriate to the situation of the particular sports tournament. Moreover, the figures that have to be analysed are not the absolute competitive-balance indicators but whether, however measured, they have changed over time so that the imposition of a policy can be assessed. There is also the issue of whether the effects on competitive balance can actually be measured. It is difficult to isolate one factor and show that it had an impact. As mentioned in the previous chapter, economists often use the phrase 'ceteris paribus', translated as 'other things being equal', but in the real world of sports, they rarely are. I am unsure that the sophistication of the calculations is matched by the evidence utilised as data in the calculations. So, although a theoretical case can be made that certain actions could influence competitive balance, empirically it is difficult to substantiate that this actually happened. My view is that unless the results are significant in one direction or the other, it is reasonable to discount them. Marginal differences cannot justify any policies. You can argue about fairies at the bottom of the garden but the presence of giants is indisputable.

Despite this (over)concentration on competitive balance and result uncertainty by economists, there are other aspects of sport which can be attractive to audiences. Product quality certainly affects demand. In their study of Spanish football, Garcia et al. (2020) suggested that quality could be considered a luxury good with a higher degree of *price and income elasticity*. They did this by estimating *hedonic prices* (ones that cannot be directly observed) and using proxies for quality (team budgets) and uncertainty of outcome (relative league positions at the time of the fixture). In passing, do not confuse (as I once did) hedonic prices with hedonistic prices, which are certainly observable for luxury goods! Even with the higher prices charged, EPL teams have larger crowds than lower division sides in the EFL, who, in turn, attract larger attendances than Sunday parkland football teams. Forrest and Simmons (2002) found that in the EFL itself, the quality of the home team (based on league position and the division played in) was a major influence on match attendance. It is possible that this could be even more important a factor in North American sports where the distribution of franchises means that away fans have large distances to travel. At the lower end of the quality scale, relegation fights may also play a role; though, of course, this does not apply to American sport. The quality of a league can be affected by talent investment and talent allocation by shifting good players, who would just be benchwarmers at one club, to a lower quality club where they would get more game time (Késenne 2015).

Quality can also be seen in the drawing power of a superstar competitor, by which an iconic sporting figure attracts more people to an event than would otherwise be the case. This is not simply a matter of comparing attendances on the days when the superstars played with those when they did not, as other factors have to be allowed for, such as the weather, day of the week, and league positions. Studies of American basketball give divergent results. Using econometric analysis and controlling for the quality of the teams involved, Hausmann and Leonard (1997) show that arena attendance in the NBA increased significantly by the on-court presence of superstar players like Michael Jordan and Shaquille O'Neal. Television audiences were similarly boosted. In contrast, Berri et al. (2004) argue that superstars had little personal appeal, and any increase in attendance can be attributed to the quality of their play, which improved a team's winning record. Whether star appeal and on-court productivity are mutually exclusive is a moot point. A major problem in both sets of calculations is that it was difficult to determine whether spectator demand had risen when basketball stadiums often sold out to full capacity. More recently, Humphreys and Johnson (2020) looked at 34,000 NBA games over a 30-year period and, after allowing for fan preference for home wins, weekday fixtures, and market catchment area, concluded that superstars do influence crowd attendance both by virtue of their talent (using player performance measures, such as points, assists, blocks) and also their popularity (using the public votes for All-Star Game representatives). They demonstrate that there were superstar effects throughout the period studied and that the effects were portable and moved with the player if he switched teams.

Compared to other elite professional sports in the United States, with no significant broadcasting contract, Major League Soccer (MLS) was initially much more dependent on gate and match-day stadium revenue. In 2007, in an effort to attract more fans to the stadiums, MLS brought in the Designated Player rule, which allowed marquee signings to be paid outside the salary cap imposed on all clubs. Jewell (2017) examined the impact of this on attendance between 2007 and 2012 and found that few such signings significantly influenced home attendance, and any strongly positive effect came in their first year. That said, marquee players raised attendance at away games (where spectators would only have one opportunity to see them) more than at the home games. This could have helped those clubs that could not afford a marquee salary and thus was in the interests of MLS, which, unlike in the other American leagues, owned all the participating clubs.

Although sports products have unique characteristics, sports spectators are like other consumers and can exhibit a preference for one product (type of sport) over another and, within that sport, for one team rather than the others. If promoters wish to penetrate deeper into the market for sport/leisure products, they need to encourage repeat buying of their particular product, as one-off purchases do not provide a firm customer base. There are two types of repeat purchasers: *repertoire buyers* and *subscription buyers*. The former satisfies their requirements for a type of product from a selection of brands, thus exhibiting polygamous loyalty in that they do not switch brands permanently. The latter allocate their spending on that type of product predominantly to one brand (Fujak et al. 2018). The relevance to sports spectators is that repertoire buyers will watch different kinds of sport, perhaps being willing to venture to a new venue, particularly if it is in a different season or features a star player. This might apply also to the supporter who has loyalty to a particular team. Promoters will be hard-pressed to persuade them to watch another team in the same competition, especially if it involves travel to a different stadium, but irregular visits to watch a different sport might be feasible. The task of the promoter is to persuade repertoire buyers to become season ticket holders, but this is not easy. A participant golfer might hold several club memberships, but, for spectators, the purchase of a season ticket reinforces their loyalty to a particular club.

Sport can be habit-forming, even addictive. One of the best guides to whether someone will attend a sports event in the future is how much they have attended in the past. What clubs and promoters need to do is create a consumer habit of watching sport, preferably by the purchase of a season ticket (*persistent habit*) but also among less regular attendees (*intermittent habit*) who might be persuaded to attend more frequently by an improvement in the quality of the product on offer. If the habit is developed, then should bad weather or other adverse circumstances deter attendance at one event, it is possible that above-average attendance might occur at the next game opportunity, as consumers, deprived of their sporting fix, seek to make up for its absence. This appears to be the case in Major League Baseball where games are more frequent than in other sports (Ge et al. 2019). Much, I suspect, depends on the gap between viewing opportunities, which must be limited enough not to weaken the habit. Hence it might also apply in first-class cricket or golf tournaments where there could be a play the following day. In Scotland, and perhaps elsewhere, during the COVID-19 lockdown, football clubs have streamed past matches at their regular kick-off times to keep fans in the viewing habit.

You Don't Have to Be There

The parameters of sports spectatorship have changed. Today, fans (or at least those with access to a subscriber channel) can watch any team in the world that has its matches televised. Moreover, television, with its instant replays, close-ups of the action, and expert punditry, now offers the home viewer something better than the best seats in the stadium. Undoubtedly it is satellite television that has made the EPL a global brand, with claimed viewing figures of 3 billion in 225 countries and about a third of its broadcasting rights money coming from international sales. The importance of local markets and physical attendance at the game has reduced, and income from broadcasting rights has become the dominant item in club accounts. Gone are the days when clubs feared that televised matches would cut attendance; gone too has the importance of gate-money for elite clubs. The money from television contracts now appears to be the driving force in many sports, which leads to the danger of the sports industry becoming too reliant on one source of revenue. Currently, competition between broadcasters is keeping income high for sports organisations, but it can go wrong. When Irish broadcaster Setanta's contract with the Scottish Football League collapsed in 2009, several clubs were placed in financial jeopardy.

Sports rights are valuable to broadcasters, as they bring in particular consumer groups which are attractive to advertisers and programme sponsors, as well as driving subscriptions to pay channels. As with all forms of intellectual property, the value to the broadcasters increases with exclusivity, scope, and duration. However, they have to compete for both the rights and the viewers. The coming of pay channels to join the traditional free-to-view ones, financed by licences or advertising revenue, has expanded the number of buyers and, in a simple working out of *supply* and *demand*, driven up the fees paid to sports organisations. This is a reversal of earlier positions when content providers competed for scarce distribution outlets (Szymanski 2006). In Europe, major sports rights have migrated to subscription channels, less so in North America where free-to-air broadcasters are allowed much more advertising time. Not all markets in sport work the same way. Spectators don't submit sealed bids for tickets or a half-time pie, but when the television rights for the EPL are on offer, broadcasters will bid that way. Such blind competitive bidding almost inevitably leads to the auction winner paying an inflated price, as all bidders are trying to beat their rivals in a once-only bid.

Several aspects of the economics of broadcast sport deserve attention. First is the issue of collective selling of rights by sports leagues rather than letting individual clubs do their own negotiations. When you have a *monopolistic* seller, a higher price can be demanded, which increases the cost to the sports consumer and can reduce their choice if the number of games televised is restricted. Collective selling is allowed in both the North American and European markets, but to protect the consumer from exploitation, European governments often insist that separate bundles of matches should be offered for auction, and in America, individual teams have the right to sell broadcast rights for local games to local broadcasters. This has allowed some clubs to do better financially than others. In 2001, for example, the Yankees generated local New York television income of $57 million, while in Montreal, the Expos garnered only $0.5 million; this is one reason why the MLB franchise was transferred to Washington, DC, in 2004.

For many sports fans, the cost of consuming broadcast sport is becoming increasingly expensive, partly because what was free-to-view keeps disappearing behind paywalls, but also, ironically, because the market for subscription channels or pay-per-view events has become more competitive. In Britain, for example, Sky used to offer the sporting world for a single subscription, but now competing channels have fragmented the market. To watch the elite rugby union costs £7.99 a month to Amazon for the Nations Cup, £9.99 to Premier Sport for the PRO14, and a joint Sky Sports and BT Sport package at £52 for European rugby, the Lions, and the English premiership. Bidding wars between the various channels have benefitted the coffers of the rugby organisations but raised the cost to the consumer to cover the prices paid. A one-stop package negotiated by a monopsonic buyer might actually have benefitted the rugby devotee. This was certainly the case with EPL football where Butler and Massey (2019) have shown that when Sky had a monopoly, the cost per game between 2000/2001 and 2006/2007 fell 29% in real terms, but when competition came in, it rose 37% (2007/2008–2012/2013), and when further competition was introduced, it rose another 28% by 2018/2019. Of course, competition between broadcasters for audiences is not necessarily on price alone. Sky Sport claims that with its pundits and in-game technology, it offers a higher quality product, and one reason why the Setanta deal collapsed was that it did not offer a substantially cheaper price, even though Scottish football was an inferior product to the EPL.

The advantage to sports leagues in selling packages is twofold. First, they can maximise revenue by having competitions for each segment and thus attract bids from broadcasters who could not contemplate bidding for the full package: in such cases, the sum of the parts will be greater than a single whole. Second, television packages can be used as a barrier to entry for competing leagues. In the 1960s, the American Football League (AFL) had challenged the NFL by securing television contracts, first with the ABC network and later with NBC. This enabled the fledgling league to survive, even though its franchises were in small cities with small crowds. The continued viability of the AFL eventually led the NFL to merge with the other organisation. A lesson had been learned and, henceforth, the NFL spread broadcasts over all three major networks, cutting off a vital source of funds for potential rival leagues, such as the World Football League in the 1970s and the United States Football League in the following decade, both of which failed primarily because of a lack of television exposure.

The previous discussion centres on the concept of *foreclosure*, which, in economic terms, is not the nasty mortgage lender taking away your house but a limitation put on a production organisation by being denied access to a supplier (*upstream foreclosure*) or to a buyer (*downstream foreclosure*). Certain upstream inputs, in our case premium quality sport, are indispensable for downstream broadcasters to compete in the market for sports fans (Hoehn and Lancefield 2003). These cannot be easily replicated without significant costs to the broadcasters, but it has been done. Feeling that they were being shut out of television contracts, the Kerry Packer organisation did this twice in Australia with World Series Cricket and the Superleague in rugby league. In both instances, rapprochement resulted in a merger of the competing competitions (reducing the outlay to produce events) and the acquisition of significant television rights. Another example of foreclosure is the vertical integration that occurs when media interests buy sports producers and supply their own products, often keeping them exclusive to themselves. In many countries, media companies own sports clubs, teams, and events, with the intention of gaining publicity for the network, a guarantee of a product to telecast, with a possible third motive in North America of capital gains from team franchises.

To a degree, the televising of sport has changed the market for sports spectatorship. Having a subscription to a sports television channel tempts fans to watch a variety of sports or even rival teams in the same competition (perhaps because of the quality of the game or a desire to see them defeated). The only short-term repeat purchase is for specific pay-per-view events, primarily boxing contests. The uncertainty hypothesis developed in the United States where the vast distances between venues meant that away supporters did not travel that much to games. In recent decades, however, television audiences have become much more important, and they can be anywhere. Are there now two demand functions for spectator sport, one centred on the stadium and the other on the box? Competitive balance may become an outdated concept in a sporting world where the greatest audiences come through broadcasting. Rising television audiences lead to a suspicion that something more than equality of competition has stimulated demand.

Berkowitz et al. (2011) analysed the 2007–2009 NASCAR seasons and found that viewers were influenced by race-level and season-level uncertainty of outcome, whereas attendees responded only to the season-level variety. Moreover, unlike physical attendance where crowd size is determined by *ex ante* (remember this is economist speak for before an event) expectations about the game – its quality, excitement, or importance – viewership can be influenced while the game is in progress and television channels switched or switched off at no cost to the viewer. Alvary et al. (2010) examined minute-by-minute television viewer ratings for EPL games and showed that the number of viewers decreased as the result became more predictable. Chung et al. (2016) looked at the Korean Professional Baseball League's 2010 season, one in which every match was televised (usually four games simultaneously), and suggested that fans responded more sensitively to the uncertainty of the game outcomes in their television viewing than in decisions on whether or not to attend. However, in Italian football, Caruso et al. (2019) suggest that fans watch their own teams by preference but otherwise opt for talent and teams at the top of the table. Such variations could have consequences for future broadcasting contracts.

We know less about the demand for televised individual sports than team sports.

- For tennis (based on German viewers 1999–2010) the preference is for prestigious competitions, significant matches (not early rounds), high-ranking players and, for these particular viewers, German ones.

  (Konjer et al. 2017)

- For golf (based on American viewers and the later rounds of 33 PGA Tour tournaments 2010–2013) the preference is for prestigious tournaments, the presence of superstars, but not uncertainty of outcome.

  (Gooding and Frank Stephenson 2017)

- For Formula 1 (based on German viewers and 400 races 1993–2014), the preference is for uncertainty of outcome based on the times of the three leading qualifiers.

(Schreger and Targler 2018)

- For road cycling, a sport that depends primarily on television, as spectators cannot be charged, and perhaps a sport that is a halfway house between individual and team, (based on Spanish viewers and 278 races/stages 2007–2011) the preference is for competitive balance, stage races, mountainous stages, and, for these particular viewers, Spanish riders.

(Rodríguez et al. 2017)

References

Alvary, Kevin, Alisson Gaskell, Stephanie Leach and Stefan Szymanski (2010), 'On the Edge of Your Seat: Demand for Football on Television and the Uncertainty of Outcome Hypothesis', *International Journal of Sport Finance* 5.2, 75–95.

Berkowitz, Jason P., Craig A. Depken and Dennis P. Wilson (2011), 'When Going in Circles Is Going Backwards: Outcome Uncertainty in NASCAR', *Journal of Sports Economics* 12.3, 253–283.

Berri, David J., Martin B. Schmidt and Stacey L. Brook (2004), 'Stars at the Game: The Impact of Star Power on NBA Gate Revenues', *Journal of Sports Economics* 5.1, 33–50.

Blackham, Julian and Bruce Chapman (2004), 'The Value of Don Bradman: Additional Revenue in Australian Ashes Tests', *Economic Papers* 23.4, 369–385.

Butler, Robert and Patrick Massey 2019, 'Has Competition in the Market for Subscription Sports Broadcasting Benefited Consumers? The Case of the English Premier League', *Journal of Sports Economics* 20.4, 603–624.

Caruso, Raul, Francesco Addesa and Marci Di Domizio (2019), 'The Determinants of the TV Demand for Soccer: Empirical Evidence on the Italian Serie A for the Period 2008–2015', *Journal of Sports Economics* 20.1, 25–49.

Chung, Jigyu, Young Hooh Lee and Joon-Ho Kang (2016), '*Ex-Ante* and *Ex-Post* Expectations of Outcome Uncertainty and Baseball Television Viewing', *Journal of Sports Economics* 17.8, 790–812.

Cox, Adam (2018), 'Spectator Demand, Uncertainty of Results, and Public Interest: Evidence From the English Premier League', *Journal of Sports Economics* 19.1, 3–30.

Forrest, David and Robert Simmons (2002), 'Outcome Uncertainty and Attendance Demand in Sport: The Case of English Soccer', *The Statistician* 51.2, 229–241.

Fujak, Hunter, Stephen Frawley, Heath McDonald and Stephen Bush, 'Are Sports Consumers Unique? Consumer Behavior within Crowded Sport Markets', *Journal of Sport Management* 32.4 (2018), 362–375.

Garcia, Jaume, Plácido Rodriguez and Federico Todeschini (2020), 'The Demand for the Characteristics of Football Matches: A Hedonic Price Approach', *Journal of Sports Economics* 21.7, 688–704.

Ge, Qi, Brad R. Humphreys and Zhou, Kun (2019), 'Are Fair Weather Fans Affected by Weather? Rainfall, Habit Formation, and Live Game Attendance', *Journal of Sports Economics* 20.3, 304–322.

Gooding, Chase and E. Frank Stephenson (2017), 'Superstars, Uncertainty of Outcome, and PGA Tour Television Ratings', *Journal of Sports Economics* 18.8, 867–875.

Gyimesi, András (2020), 'League Ranking Mobility Affects Attendance: Evidence From European Soccer Leagues', *Journal of Sport Economics* 21.8, 808–828.

Hausmann, Jerry A. and Gregory K. Leonard (1997). 'Superstars in the National Basketball Association: Economic Value and Policy', *Labor Economics* 15.4, 586–624.

Hoehn, Tom and David Lancefield (2003), 'Broadcasting and Sport', *Oxford Review of Economic Policy* 19.4, 552–568.

Humphreys, Brad R. and Candon Johnson (2020), 'The Effect of Superstars on Game Attendance: Evidence From the NBA', *Journal of Sports Economics* 21.2, 152–175.

Humphreys, Brad R. and Thomas J. Miceli (2019), 'The Peculiar Preferences of Sports Fans: Toward a Preference-Based Motivation for the Uncertainty of Outcome Hypothesis', *Journal of Sports Economics* 20.6, 782–796.

Jewell, R. Todd (2017), 'The Effect of Marquee Players on Sports Demand: The Case of U.S. Major League Soccer', *Journal of Sports Economics* 18.3, 239–352.

Késenne, Stefan (2015), 'Revenue Sharing and Absolute League Quality: Talent Investment and Talent Allocation', *Scottish Journal of Political Economy* 62.1, 51–58.

Konjer, Mara, Henk Erik Meier and Katrin Wedeking (2017), 'Consumer Demand for Telecasts of Tennis Matches in Germany', *Journal of Sports Economics* 18.4, 351–375.

Lee, Young Hoon and Rodney Fort (2012), 'Competitive Balance: Time Series Lessons From the English Premier League', *Scottish Journal of Political Economy* 59. 3, 266–282.

Rodríguez, César, Levi Perez, Víctor Puente and Plácido Rodríguez (2017), 'The Determinants of Television Audience for Professional Cycling: The Case of Spain', *Journal of Sport Economics* 16.1, 26–58.

Schreger, Dominick and Benno Targler (2018), 'On the Role of Race Outcome Uncertainty in the TV Demand for Formula 1 Grands Prix', *Journal of Sports Economics* 19.2, 211–229.

Szymanski, Stefan (2006), 'The Economic Evolution of Sport and Broadcasting', *Australian Economic Review* 39.4, 428–434.

Szymanski, Stefan (2010), *Football Economics and Policy* (Palgrave Macmillan: Basingstoke).

8

SEEKING PROFIT OR UTILITY

Objectives of Owners and Entrepreneurs

Profit or Utility Revisited

Those in charge of sports organisations, especially clubs at the elite end of the sport, face the dilemma of whether their primary objective should be to make money (profit-maximisation) or to try and achieve some other non-pecuniary objective, such as winning as many games as possible and challenging for cups and championships (utility-maximisation). This is an oversimplification, but it suits the purposes of analysis. In practice, there will be a spectrum with owners veering towards the profit end or the utility end. We should also note that, as elsewhere in life, having objectives is not the same as achieving them.

The idea that profit-maximisation was not the raison d'être of professional team sports was first theorised by Sloane (1971) and made mathematical by Quirk and El Hodiri (1974), with these authors conceptualising the alternative behaviour as utility-maximisation. Over time, the concept has been amended and extended to include a variety of non-profit-maximising objectives, including a level of acceptable profit (i.e. some form of profit constraint above the break-even point), revenue-maximisation (getting more spectators through the gates, perhaps exploiting price elasticity of demand), or ownership by superfans often referred to in the American literature as 'sportsmen owners' in which spending on the club is regarded more as consumption rather than investment activity (Fort 2015).

Profit-maximisation and utility-maximisation are incompatible. Those who wish to win will want to field the best team that they can. This means spending on the best quality players they can afford. So, within the budget constraint of remaining solvent, as much money as possible will be expended on the playing squad. In contrast, the profit-seeker will be aware that the surplus achieved is the result of two variables: revenue minus costs. At some stage, spending on the team will eat too much into the potential profit and a line will be drawn on expenditure. Ah, I can hear your brains

DOI: 10.4324/9781003128632-8

ticking over: won't a winning team attract more fans and increase revenue? No, not according to most economists who, as we saw in the previous chapter, argue that crowds are maximised by competitive balance and uncertainty of outcome.

As a sweeping generalisation, utility-seekers are willing to accept long-term losses in the hope of achieving playing success. These losses are accumulated from such behaviours as hiring too large a playing squad and paying them too much (i.e. more than the revenue they bring in) and selling tickets at a discount in order to maximise team support. (If the ownership structure is a joint-stock company, this behaviour will be limited, as shareholder interests set a constraint on losses that the company can deliberately incur.) Profit-seekers are more likely to accept curbs on their behaviour by the leagues as the rational way to progress. Hence they will agree to such policies as a draft for players and also revenue sharing, both intended to improve the quality of the poorer-performing teams and as reserve clauses and salary caps, which will also serve that purpose while simultaneously reducing costs. Plumley et al. (2017) point out that sports performance and financial performance are not mutually exclusive and can actually be interrelated. Their research on the EPL demonstrates that a strong revenue stream is important to on-field performance. This is not revolutionary: the traditional argument has never been that revenue is unimportant but was concerned with whether it was expended on improving the team or taken by the owners as profit.

Ownership Motivation

The basic structural difference in ownership is that of concentrated ownership (with a single or just a few owners) and a more dispersed version (with many shareholders or even fan-based ownership).

Individually owned franchises have dominated the North American team-sport scene. These have generally been regarded by economists as profit-maximising in intent. Vrooman (2000) has suggested that there may have been some sporting success motivation at work, as when an owner comes to sell the franchise; this has often been preceded by a lowering of the talent quality in the squad (with a consequent fall in wage costs and rise in profitability) in order to inflate the value of the franchise. Nevertheless, franchises always seem to have made a capital gain, which suggests a long-term profit motive at work. Since the later twentieth century, many individually owned franchises have been superseded by syndicated ownership, though usually with limited numbers participating. Vrooman argues that this could allow any individual with a controlling interest to take a sporting success line, as less of their own money would be at risk, though he produces no hard evidence of this happening.

Hersch and Pelkowski (2019) examine the consequences of ownership change (when an outside entity purchases a majority interest in an MLB franchise) by looking at 40 such substantive occurrences between 1985 and 2014. Their major finding was that it has little impact on team performance, though one likely effect is the sacking of the general manager (odds on this rise by 177%) and club manager (206%). However, the thing most likely to follow ownership change is a modification of the club logo (249%), scarcely what disgruntled fans calling for change might have desired!

In the European sports market, too much attention has been paid to football, to the detriment of studies on other team sports, which may skew findings on the objectives of ownership. Nevertheless, researchers have not yet provided sufficient evidence to undermine the prevailing view that European owners are more concerned with on-field performance than with making money to spend on non-sports-related consumption. From their beginnings, professional sport organisations in Europe accepted control of the sport from the existing amateur governing bodies, a contrast with the United States, which may have underlined the lack of emphasis on commercial considerations. This partly stemmed from most European sports clubs beginning as membership organisations, a feature which continued to exert an influence, even when they adopted professionalism. For example, in the United Kingdom, many membership clubs had become non-quoted, joint-stock companies before 1914, but often, in essence, members simply became shareholders, maintaining both their fan support and voting rights. Over time, these companies became the fiefdom of individuals, often local businessmen, though ones generally seeking community kudos rather than direct profits.

Such *benefactor* models have now become the norm at the elite level but with the difference that the owners are rarely now local, and the kudos that are being sought are more international. This began with Russian billionaire Roman Abramovich's purchase of Chelsea in 2003, which heralded the development of a 'benefactor' model of foreign ownership in which the motive of short-term playing success outweighed financial considerations. Money does not automatically buy success, but it makes it more likely. By 2010, nine extant EPL clubs were overseas-owned, a figure that had risen to 14 before the end of the next decade. This expansion of foreign ownership tied in with the British government's acceptance, if not encouragement, of inward investment in the economy generally, and has been aided by British clubs, unlike many continental ones, being companies rather than membership associations (Vamplew 2017). In passing, governments and economists should ask themselves why inward investment is considered a 'good thing'. Historically, it wasn't for many inhabitants of formal and informal empires.

An EPL club debt burden of €3.3 billion by 2014, the bulk owed to the club owners, and an emerging similar situation elsewhere in Europe, led UEFA to introduce Financial Fair Play (FFP) rules to restrict excessive lending and spending by billionaire owners, bring a semblance of a more level playing field, and encourage clubs to live within their means (as determined by their revenue streams; Plumley et al. 2017). This came at a time when net losses among the 734 European member clubs had increased by 760% between 2006 and 2011 (Plumley et al. 2021). What the regulations have done is cement the position of the existing benefactor establishment in limiting the challenge of any newcomers: no insurgent can come in and spend significantly more than those already there (as did Sheikh Mansour in 2008 when he bought Manchester City for £210 million and has been prepared to stand annual losses of over £500 million). Such owners might not be making serious operating profits, but, as with American franchises, there are capital gains to be had. Mansour's Manchester City holding is now worth over £2 billion. However, these gains come from an asset structure with weak underpinning. They exist because there is a demand for club ownership by some extremely wealthy individuals who want the publicity, the public acclaim, and the global cachet. This demand survived the international financial crash of the noughties, but will it be adversely affected by the post-corona virus economy? And what about the product they are purchasing: will the EPL continue to retain its strong preference for the spending of these benefactors on their executive toys?

Sports clubs rarely involve themselves in vertical and horizontal integration, except in respect of farm teams and sports academies, but they themselves can be part of the investment portfolios of major companies, partly to aid industrial relations but also to benefit indirectly economically and politically from the publicity. Examples can be found in continental Europe, including Bayer Leverkusen (Bayer Pharmaceuticals), Eindhoven (Phillips Electrical), and Juventus (Fiat Cars). In Indian Premier League cricket, five of the current eight franchise holders are corporate bodies, and several Asian professional sports clubs have opted for corporate ownership, including most of those in the Japanese and Korean baseball leagues and the Chinese football league. Although many of these clubs are loss makers, the corporations keep them going as useful vehicles for publicity and community relations (Jang and Lee 2016). However, should the owners themselves run into financial trouble, the clubs could fall victim to corporate cuts as had recently occurred in Chinese football. In 2020, 16 football clubs in the top three divisions in China went out of business, including Jiangsu, which, only three months before, had won the Super League title. This was partly because their corporate owners were suffering due to the downturn in the Chinese economy. It did not help their survival when the Chinese Football Association (FA) decided to remove corporate names from club titles, thus simultaneously removing the main reason for corporate involvement.

In Spain, Brazil, and Germany, elite teams have long been owned by their members, and in the past couple of decades, there has been a move in British football towards supporters trusts in which fans buy out the owners and establish a trust to finance ownership of the team themselves, a reversion to the early days of elite football when most clubs were members' organisations. However, the amount of money that fans can raise collectively cannot match the fortunes of the benefactor owners. The best that teams owned by supporters trusts can hope for is survival, an occasional triumph in the lower echelons of their sport, and beating their local rivals. Indeed, keeping afloat may be the real motivation for supporter ownership. If the club is a big-city one, there is the possibility (not probability) of imitating such membership clubs as Real Madrid and Barcelona. In Spain, despite more corporate structures (if still non-profit in orientation) elsewhere in La Liga, two of the major football clubs, Barcelona and Real Madrid, remain membership organisations, the latter with over 50,000 members who vote in the club president. Much finance comes in the form of long-term bank loans which seem to be continually rolled over because of the cultural significance of the clubs (Dobson and Goddard 2004). More realistic a proposition might be to adopt the German model where teams in the Bundesliga have to have a minimum fan ownership of 50% plus one so that voting rights (which are one member, one vote) remain dominated by the fan base (Bauers et al. 2020). The idea is to prevent one individual or a company from taking over the club and running it in their interests (which might involve increased commercialisation) rather than those of the fans. Outside money might be welcome, but power is not to be ceded. Exceptions were allowed where companies had a long-standing relationship (20 years or more) with a club, which accounts for Bayer Leverkusen (Bayer Pharmaceuticals), Vfl Wolfsburg (Volkswagen), and, controversially, TSG Hoffenheim (run by Dietmar Hopp, an individual who has financed the club throughout its rise from the sixth tier of German football).

There has been one serious attempt in the United Kingdom to float clubs on the stock market with the implication that shareholders would seek dividends. Tottenham had pioneered this in 1983 when it raised £3.3 million (scarcely enough to buy the left toe of a star striker today but considered big money in those days), followed by Millwall's £4.8 million in 1989 and Manchester United's £6.7 million two years later. However, it was the formation of the EPL in 1992 that really kicked on the joint-stock movement in football, helped perhaps by the three and fourfold rise in the value of Spurs and Manchester United shares. By the mid-1990s, nearly half the EPL had adopted this funding mechanism, and some 15 clubs in all were floated between 1995 and 1997. In 2001, nine extant members of the EPL were listed companies, but nine years later, the figure had fallen to just two: city institutions behind the flotations had come to terms with the fact that football clubs were not attractive investments for those seeking financial returns, either as dividends or capital gains (Vamplew 2017). Leach and Szymanski (2015) suggest that as the financial behaviour of the floated clubs did not change significantly, then, given that as companies they were beholden to their shareholders, perhaps profit-seeking had been more prevalent than previously thought. To my mind, a more likely explanation is that the city made money via launching shares to gullible fans (from across the socio-economic strata) who wanted a stake in their club. These shareholders were not seeking economic returns and indeed supported the fresh capital being spent on players, just what a utility-maximiser would do.

One development in sports finance to keep an eye on is the move of private equity capital companies into sports organisations, primarily tournaments and events which require little infrastructure ownership by the financiers themselves. In May 2020, such a firm, CVC Capital Partners, paid Celtic Rugby £120 million for a 28% share in the PRO14 tournament. CVC had already been involved in sport. In 1998, it had purchased Dorna, a Spanish sports management company with exclusive rights to run the international motorcycling series MotoGP, for $80 million, but, under orders from the European Competition Commission, had sold this in 2006 for $400 million when it secured a controlling interest in Formula 1 for £1.4 billion. It retained this until 2017 when it sold out for £8 billion. In 2018, CVC paid English Premiership Rugby £200 million for a 27% stake in its tournament. It had wanted a controlling interest of 51%, but the clubs turned that down. Perhaps they were wise. It is clear that CVC has done well financially in the capital gains it has made from sport, though this might suggest that making money was its driving force rather than the long-term interests of the sports themselves. Additionally, some commentators feel that, during their time at Formula I, they extracted as much money as they could (in 2014, the return on their funding was more than 350%!) and put in as little as possible. At the time of writing, CVC is finalising a £365 million deal for a 14% share in the Six Nations Rugby and has expressed an interest in investing in Italian Serie A football. We await developments but note that CVC controls some $75 billion of funds, so it needs PRO14 and its fellow sports organisations less than they need it. New Zealand Rugby has decided to sell 12.5% of its commercial rights (via a newly created entity) to an American private equity fund, Silver Lake, for NZ$387 million. Silver Lake already holds a 10% stake in the City Football Group, which owns Manchester City. The funding will enable New Zealand Rugby to give momentum to the grassroots game, which had been hit by the national body's reduced budget during the COVID-19 pandemic. There is a somewhat naïve belief within New Zealand Rugby that the limited holding will prevent the California-based company from taking all the major commercial decisions and that they will not influence other policy aspects. Sports organisations need to realise that financiers are not altruists: always read the small print.

What most leagues do not like is multiple club ownership within the same league structure, as it calls into question the integrity of the sporting competition. A surprising, but to my mind dubiously ethical, exception is that the PRO14 rugby tournament allows the Scottish Rugby Union to own both Edinburgh and Glasgow clubs, surely a hostage to fortune when a conflict of interest inevitably arises. Generally, ownership of more than one club or franchise in the same competition is frowned on by the sport authorities and treated with suspicion by fans. Inter-country multiple ownership is less of a problem so, although the EPL prohibits its members from owning farm teams within England, there is no formal objection to Manchester City taking a stake in several clubs overseas, which they use to bring along players not yet ready for the EPL. There are similar intercontinental arrangements by several leading European football teams. Within countries, many clubs develop close relationships with other teams to the extent of regularly loaning them players. American baseball is the exemplar in that most clubs have affiliate arrangements with a host of clubs stretching from the top-level AAA down to the lowest leagues, which are used for the training and development of potential MLB players, as well as a recuperating base for injured or out-of-form major leaguers.

To Market, To Market: Sports Entrepreneurs

Owners may be businessmen but they are not necessarily sports entrepreneurs, the people who push the sports industry forwards. Traditionally, sports entrepreneurs have been seen as looking to make money from organising sport, owning teams, or marketing equipment and facilities. However, Vamplew (2018) recently loosened the straitjacket of neoclassical economic delineation and suggested a wider definition of the sports entrepreneur to encompass all who act as change agents in the supply of sports products, who attempt to increase the output of the industry, improve the consumer experience, or raise interest in sports products by such means as developing new markets and creating new products. Under this definition, no supplier of player, spectator, or associated sports products can be considered sports entrepreneurs unless they add to the supply of sport or improve the perceived quality of the sporting experience. To be an entrepreneur involves not merely running a business but risk-taking and/or innovating by, among other things, developing new sports, events, or competitions; applying new technology to the production of equipment and apparel; promoting new venues; bringing sport to new audiences and participants; making deals to have sport broadcast and televised; and reinvigorating and restructuring traditional or established areas of sport. Hence, the new definition will not include those businessmen who initially demonstrated entrepreneurship but subsequently opted to coast along rather than innovating further. This is not a criticism of their behaviour, merely a definitional elaboration: they are still economic agents but not agents of change.

The definition also says nothing about the qualities required to be a successful entrepreneur: merely to attempt is to be entrepreneurial. There is no entrepreneurial instruction book that guarantees success. Previously successful individuals and enterprises can make mistakes, and even government-backed ventures can have the plug pulled on them. The literature focuses on the successful entrepreneurs and pays little heed to those ventures that failed, yet, if risk-taking is a quality of entrepreneurs, there must have been failures. As in sport, business too perhaps had more failures than successes, but, regrettably, in neither sphere have they been adequately researched. The history of sports entrepreneurship is full of such examples, and they should not be ignored when we trace the development of sport, as the failures may have pushed sport to develop in particular ways.

In many ways, sports entrepreneurs are no different from other entrepreneurs in that they are concerned with strategic planning, talent acquisition, and public relations, but there are some differences stemming from sport being a special form of industry due to the nature of the sport product and its economics not always being congruent with those of more conventional business. To make the concept of sports entrepreneurship more meaningful and less complex, let us look at entrepreneurship by objective. I identify four categories of entrepreneurs, each with several subcategories. First, there are those who seek profits or non-salary income directly from sport. The most common of these are the producers/sellers of equipment and apparel and those who promote a sports event and charge spectators to see it. The latter are not always conventional sports promoters but can include those who put on events to raise money for charity and also sports professionals who run the various tennis and golf tours. Then there are 'sports entertainment' entrepreneurs who promote events in which the sport itself is secondary to the entertainment value being marketed (as in professional wrestling). The entrepreneurs here believe that the entertainment value of normal sport is not enough, so they emphasise the spectacle. Nor should we forget what I term 'dark entrepreneurs', those who corrupted sport or tarnished its image for economic ends but who, in doing so, attracted audiences and improved the quality of the performances witnessed. They may have undermined or even destroyed the integrity of a sport, but clearly, they were still innovators. Among the dark entrepreneurs are the sports goods corporations and the Pakistani middlemen who make profits from the labour of young children hand-stitching footballs and those who supply drugs so that athletes can improve their performances.

Second, we have those entrepreneurs who also seek revenue from sport but indirectly. These include sports promoters who are more concerned with the catering and drink franchises; those who sponsor events so as to publicise their line of business or, as with the media, to increase circulation or attract viewers (which then allows them to attract advertisers); and those local authorities who supply sports facilities to tempt tourists to their locale. Another set of income-seekers who promote gate-money sport have the primary intention of creating a vehicle for gambling. Sport and gambling can work well together; having a bet can add to the excitement of the event, and the unpredictability of sport can create a lively betting market.

A third group of entrepreneurs seek *psychic income* and personal or national kudos from sport. Their efforts can result in profits, but that is not their driving force. Some of this, as with civic boosterism, brings in the concept of the public good. This refers not to the supplier but to the consumer. If the use of a product is exclusive, then it is a private good; but, if it can be enjoyed by many without excluding other users, then it is a public good. Economists use the example of a lighthouse whose light cannot be restricted solely to paying customers. Governments often invest in elite sport, as they feel that, although their citizens may not be able to get tickets to the Olympics (private good), they can bask in the reflected glory of gold medals won by their nation's athletes (public good). This did, of course, in the case of East Germany lead to dark entrepreneurship in the form of the state-sanctioned use of performance-enhancing drugs. 'Putting the nation on the map' is a slogan used to justify devoting taxpayers' money to the hosting of mega-events. In a similar vein, many American city authorities use public funds to attract or retain a big-league team franchise by building new stadia or reconstructing old ones. Although sport, especially soccer, is sometimes used in Britain as a vehicle for charity fundraising, many of those promoting or sponsoring events gained personal kudos from their involvement. Such kudos may also be a motive of team owners who seek to maximise utility; in non-economic terms, they put winning trophies before making money. This is not to infer that they might not make a surplus, simply that this is not their dominant aim.

Finally, there are those with specifically *not-for-profit* objectives. Such entrepreneurs may not always be operating in a free-market economy. Many might have been supplying intermediate goods with the intention of using sport to achieve some non-sport goal, be it municipal authorities providing swimming baths for health purposes, recreational groups (perhaps with religious, political, or racial ties) forming sports clubs with social capital formation or conviviality in mind, or the armed forces making sport compulsory as preparation for military service.

Whereas Vamplew emphasised entrepreneurial objectives, Porter (2019) focused on the process of entrepreneurship. He viewed sports entrepreneurs as innovators who disrupt the market and suggested that the creative process of entrepreneurship could be analysed as the emergence of new combinations of products and promoters, proposing three categories: *parasitic*, *strategic*, and *symbiotic*. Parasitic sports entrepreneurs are those who tag onto sports events to sell their wares but have no specific connections to sport and could attach themselves to any crowd-drawing occasion. Strategic combinations involve striking a structural relationship between sport and non-sport business activities, such as jewellers moving into trophy manufacture or fashion houses designing sportswear. Symbiotic combinations are conceived within the sports sector with various parts of the sports product, be it player, spectator, or associated, being brought together to create something new.

References

Bauers, Sebastian Björn, Joachim Lammert, Axel Faix and Gregor Hovemann (2020), 'Club Members in German Professional Football and Their Attitudes to the 50+1 Rule: A Stakeholder-Oriented Analysis', *Soccer & Society* 21.3, 274–288.

Dobson, Stephen and John Goddard (2004), 'Ownership and Finance of Professional Soccer in England and Europe' in Rodney Fort and John Fizel (eds.), *International Sports Economics Comparisons* (Praeger: Westport, CT), 189–206.

Fort, Rodney (2015), 'Managerial Objectives: A Retrospective on Utility Maximisation in Pro Team Sports', *Scottish Journal of Political Economy* 62.1, 75–89.

Hersch, Philip L. and Jodi E. Pelkowski (2019), 'The Consequences (and Nonconsequences) of Ownership Changes: The Case of Major League Baseball', *Journal of Sports Economics* 20.1, 72–90.

Jang, Hayley and Young Hoon Lee (2016), 'A Business Analysis of Asian Baseball Leagues', *Asian Economic Policy Review* 11, 95–112.

Leach, Stephanie and Stefan Szymanski (2015), 'Making Money Out of Football', *Scottish Journal of Political Economy* 62.1, 25–50.

Plumley, Daniel, Jean-Philippe Serbera and Rob Wilson (2021), 'Too Big to Fail: Accounting for Prediction of Financial Distress in English Professional Football Clubs', *Journal of Applied Accounting* 22.1, 93–113.

Plumley, Daniel, Robert Wilson and Simon Shibli (2017), 'A Holistic Performance Assessment of English Premier League Football Clubs 1992–2013', *Journal of Applied Sports Management* 9.1, 1–24.

Porter, Dilwyn (2019), 'Opportunistic, Parasitic, Strategic, Symbiotic: Entrepreneurship and the Business of Sport' in Dilwyn Porter and Wray Vamplew (eds.), *Sport and Entrepreneurship* (Routledge: Abingdon), 19–36.

Quirk, J. and M. El Hodiri (1974), 'The Economic Theory of a Professional Sports League' in R.G. Noll (ed.), *Government and the Sports Business* (Brookings Institute: Washington), 33–80.

Sloane, Peter J. (1971), 'The Economics of Professional Football: The Football Club as a Utility Maximiser', *Scottish Journal of Political Economy* 18.2, 121–146.

Vamplew, Wray (2017), 'Creating the English Premier Football League: A Brief Economic History with Some Possible Lessons for Asian Soccer', *International Journal of the History of Sport* 34.17–18, 1807–1818.

Vamplew, Wray (2018), 'Products, Promotion and (Possibly) Profits: Sports Entrepreneurship Revisited', *Journal of Sport History* 45.2, 183–201.

Vrooman, John (2000), 'The Economics of American Sports Leagues', *Scottish Journal of Political Economy* 47.4, 364–398.

9

TOURNAMENTS AND LEAGUES

Tournaments

Designing an optimal contest is a matter of significant financial concern for the organisers and participants but also a matter of consuming personal interest for fans (Szymanski 2003).

It is imperative that tournament organisers structure their events so that participants are not given incentives to underperform. Preston and Szymanski (2003) note two instances where tournament design enabled teams to perform to their advantage in a manner contrary to the spirit of the game but within the rules of the event. In the 1994 Shell Caribbean (Football) Cup, the rules stated that a win in extra time would be counted as a two-goal victory, so when Barbados, needing a two-goal margin to progress to the final, were only two to one up with just minutes remaining, the team deliberately kicked the ball into their own net to force overtime. Five years later, in the Cricket World Cup, the regulations said that teams which advanced to the second stage carried with them any points they had gained from matches with opponents who also progressed. Hence, when Australia played West Indies, the Australian team deliberately slowed down their scoring so that, although they won and gained the points on offer, they also guaranteed that the West Indies team went through by virtue of their net run rate aided by the Aussies' beneficence. Using a complex theoretical exposition, Dagaev and Sonin (2018) argue that there is an inherent design flaw in any tournament where qualification can come from two different competitions in which the same competitors play, such as in the various national football leagues and cups, both of which can lead to entry into lucrative European competitions. The qualifications are non-cumulative in that no club can qualify twice for the same tournament, so, in certain circumstances, a team might consider whether it is better to qualify from one competition or the other, particularly as this decision might adversely affect the fortunes of

DOI: 10.4324/9781003128632-9

bitter rivals. In other words, there is an incentive to play strategically not to win. Although the authors stress that this is a low probability occurrence, it is still a potential integrity issue.

More generally, tournament organisers have to ensure that the reward structure is such that it can attract sufficient quality players and give them an incentive to try their best. The function of prize money seems obvious: to the winner goes the spoils. Yet experience showed that winner-takes-all style tournaments did not bring in sufficient quality competitors to be an attraction for spectators or broadcasting companies. One-offs might be successful, as in the 2018 skins golf match between Americans Phil Mickelson and Tiger Woods, but they do not create sustained public interest. A balance has to be struck between this and sharing the prize money out equally, which would remove the economic incentive to win. This seems to have been worked out both in NASCAR races (Allmen 2001; Schwartz et al. 2007) and on the American PGA tour (Shmanske 2007) where studies of late-twentieth-century events have shown that the differentials in prize money are sufficient for those who might not win still to perform as well as they can.

The reward system in golf is designed to keep players trying until the last shot. Apart from the occasional high-profile skins game and appearance money paid to attract star players, most money in golf is earned from stroke-play events, usually played over four rounds with a cut at the halfway point to eliminate the poorer-performing golfers. All those who make the cut gain prize money, with the winner getting the largest slice. Hence, even when they cannot win, a player can earn more money by moving up the scoreboard. Conversely not trying their best towards the end of their last round could prove expensive. Unlike in team sports, where end-of-season matches can be meaningless for some clubs, in golf, any player can still triumph in the last tournaments of the year, though recently these events have been reserved for the best performing players during the season. Even here, however, on the US PGA Tour, the fields are consecutively reduced to 90, 60, and 30 players for the last three events of the season with massive prize money at stake.

Leagues

Most competitive professional team sports are organised through leagues, which can be seen as joint ventures in which clubs (as businesses) pool their complementary assets and capabilities to gain integrative efficiencies and share risks (Flynn and Gilbert 2001). Traditionally, leagues in the United States have been unincorporated associations comprising their respective clubs, which can be individually owned, partnerships, or corporations. However, in the past two decades, new leagues in North America have organised as a single corporate entity, with the team owners having a financial stake in the league itself and the league actually owning the contracts of players (Flynn and Gilbert 2001). The constituent clubs in leagues usually have the discretion to set admission prices, market their own games, and adopt strategies to compete with other clubs in the playing area. Other decisions are taken by the league as a whole, and this is a major exercise in economic design encompassing competition rules, league structure and composition, revenue regulation and allocation, organisation of the labour market, and determining acceptable ownership. This competition on the field with simultaneous cooperation off it is an example of what is termed *coopetition*, an inelegant concept covering cooperation between competing companies that form a strategic alliance designed to help both businesses.

What leagues can do is reduce what economists term *transaction costs* for clubs in scheduling fixtures and negotiating broadcasting contracts. Transaction costs are those in addition to the price paid and can be direct financial costs or implicit ones associated with time or inconvenience. They generally fall into one of three major categories:

- Search and information costs involved in finding out about the relevant market
- Bargaining and decision costs involved in negotiating a deal
- Policing and enforcement costs involved in ensuring that you get what you negotiated or paid for

The essence of league survival and sustainability is mutual interdependence and the acceptance by constituent clubs of regulations imposed by the leagues, though there is still a need for mechanisms to enforce them. As member organisations, they often operate on a principle of 'one member, one vote', which can produce resistance to change unless the body has strong leadership. Economic self-interest can often rule: recently in Scottish football, a vote was taken on abandoning the current season and determining positions on average points per game thus far; those clubs fearing relegation or losing prize money rankings opted to support the resolution. Two clubs, Heart of Midlothian and Partick Thistle, were consequently relegated from their respective divisions, even though the latter had a game in hand over the team two points above them. Astute readers, who know of my Hibernian allegiance, might note that I say nothing about the fairness or otherwise of the decision involving the Hearts. A proposal by the Hearts to restructure the league to avoid all relegations and bring in two non-league teams whose promotion had been thwarted secured only 16 votes out of a possible 42. Too many clubs felt that the prize money pool would be diluted and, for those in the premiership, financially valuable fixtures against the Rangers and Celtic would be reduced in number. The importance of the Celtic and Rangers to Scottish football is enshrined in the premiership itself, where two votes (from 12 clubs) against any motion is sufficient to defeat any proposals: democracy in action!

The main economic criticism of leagues is that they act as *cartels* (something illegal in conventional business), behaving uncompetitively and consequently reducing *economic welfare* for sports consumers (usually by them having to pay higher prices for their entertainment). This raises the issue of what is an appropriate/acceptable level of cooperation between teams within a professional sports league. Clearly not match-fixing but certainly match scheduling. However, deciding mutually who could or could not be a member and which centres of population can host a franchise are questionable, as they have effects both on those excluded and also on existing franchises. A vital point is that the lessening of economic competition between league members can be offset by benefits to consumers simply because without that collaboration, there might be no league at all, which would be a massive loss in economic welfare. If an oil cartel is broken up, then consumers might benefit from cheaper petrol, but if a league is dismantled, there is no product to be consumed.

Open Leagues

A major decision to be made is whether to be an open league with membership determined by promotion and relegation or a closed league where membership is guaranteed. Szymanski (2004) has noted several economic features of the promotion and relegation system.

- While it can promote uncertainty and keep teams playing to win till the end of the season, both possibly adding to the interests of the consumer, simultaneously, it may undermine the motivation to invest in infrastructure and facilities if even medium-term survival cannot be guaranteed.
- Such a precarious situation in which a club cannot promise participation in the top league also lessens the ability of a club to secure *economic rents* by threatening to relocate the franchise elsewhere.
- It can undermine profitability, as owners spend on players in an attempt to avoid relegation.
- Finally, and perhaps theoretically, it can lead to inefficient economic outcomes with a major city not having a team that competes at the highest level while smaller towns with poorly supported teams (in terms of crowd sizes) do: this reduces the overall spectator satisfaction as fewer people in aggregate watch the games.

One aspect of *competitive balance* that has rarely been investigated is the parachute payments given for three years to clubs that are relegated from the EPL (unless they are promoted in that period, as otherwise, the definition of a parachute would have to be changed!). In 2016/2017, the amounts paid were £42 million in the first year, followed by £34 million, and then £15 million. Similar, but less generous, payments also occur in the major football leagues of Italy, Austria, and Denmark but not in either the Bundesliga or La Liga. Although all English championship clubs (the level immediately below the EPL) received solidarity payments that season of £4.5 million from the EPL (in essence crumbs from the rich man's table), these were less than a sixth of the parachute payments (funded from broadcasting revenues) designed to ease the financial distress of the dramatic fall in revenue after leaving the EPL. In 2015, these payments accounted for half the aggregate revenues of the ten clubs in receipt of them (before you ask, it was ten, as the financial year and the football year do not coincide). Laudable though these payments are, they do give the clubs concerned a decided financial advantage over their rivals in the championship. Wilson et al. (2018) have examined 11 seasons from 2006/2007 and found that clubs with parachute payments were twice as likely to gain promotion and considerably less likely to be relegated to the third tier of English football. They claimed that this led to a 'moderately strong (sic) decline in competitive balance', but this appears to be one of less than 4% over 11 years. I would argue that, as almost half the clubs were receiving parachute payments at one time, this still allowed for significant competition between those clubs.

Closed Leagues

Quality control by promotion and relegation has never appealed to the Americans, who feel the loss in asset value of a franchise would be too large a price to pay. Instead, they operate closed leagues where clubs are guaranteed places. Any changes in league composition come via the moving of a franchise to another city or the adding of new franchises. The former is a decision taken by the franchise owner who has the liberty to accept an offer from another city or to sell the franchise to another owner from another city. The latter is subject to the permission of the existing teams that obtain a share of the fee charged to the newcomer. This has not proven to be an insurmountable barrier, as between 1960 and 1999, the MLB expanded from 16 to 30 clubs, the NFL from 13 to 31, the NBA from 8 to 29, and the NHL from 6 to 27. Closed leagues were initially instigated in Japanese football, but once the J-League was successfully established, promotion and relegation between its two divisions were instituted, though no club faced relegation out of the overall league structure (Dolles and Söderman 2005/2006). There is a growing economic pressure for closed leagues to be adopted in some British sports, but currently, this is counterbalanced by the argument that relegation battles attract crowds.

In many closed leagues, attempts to maintain spectator interest throughout the season come from determining the title by an end-of-season, play-off system in which even teams well down the league ladder could participate, though usually with more games to play to qualify for the final than those who performed better all season. One of the most surprising play-offs was in the Australian Football League Grand Final of 2016 when seventh-place finishers, Western Bulldogs, ended a 62-year premiership drought with a 22-point victory over minor premiers, the Sydney Swans.

However, in trying to strike a balance of keeping as much fan interest in the competition for as long as possible while not penalising too much those clubs which have performed best throughout the first stages, rules have sometimes become convoluted. Prior to 2011, Super Rugby (at that time involving teams from South Africa, Australia, and New Zealand) was a round-robin competition in which each team played every other team once. The top four teams at the end of the round-robin phase then played semi-finals – the first-place team hosted the fourth-place team, and the second-place team hosted the third-placed team The two winners then played the final at the home ground of the top surviving seed. All well and good, but then between 2011 and 2015, the format changed, with each country having its own conference within which each team played each of the other teams twice, once at home and once away. Now it becomes more complicated. Each team then played four out of the five teams from each of the other conferences once. The format of the finals also changed, as it involved six teams: the top team in each of the three conferences plus the three next teams with the highest total number of points, regardless of conference. The four lower ranking teams of the six finalists were paired in two sudden death games; the winners of those two games each then played one of the two top-ranked teams (which received a bye at the start of the finals). Those winners played for the championship. Now forget all that, as for the next two seasons, the format changed again, with three more teams joining, one each from Argentina, Japan, and South Africa. Now there were four conferences based on two regional groups with five teams in both the New Zealand and Australian conferences and two South African conferences which included a team from Japan and one from Argentina. The finals had eight teams, with each conference winner getting a home quarter-final. They were joined by four wild card teams, three from the Australasian group and one from the South African group. Having just got your minds around that, it changed again in 2018 to a three-conference system based on geography but with Japan added to the Australian group and Argentina retained as part of the South African one. And guess what, it changed again after that, but I won't confuse you with any more details.

Expansion and Contraction

Business always wants to expand, and the sports business is no different. Hence the Olympics has become a huge global enterprise; the World Cups in football, cricket, and rugby have all increased the number of teams reaching the final stages; football teams no longer have to win their premierships to enter the Champions League, and the first event of the European 2019 PGA tour was in November 2018 in Hong Kong, with sports business here taking both geographical and chronological liberties. Irrespective of the circumstances, leagues, too, want to grow in asset value, in revenue turnover, and, especially, in market reach. The stationary state is not for them. Many leagues (or rather their membership) have such ambitions to expand. In this, they are no different from many business organisations that want to grow and make more money. Some, however, may have wished they had been content to remain as the corner shop.

A prime example of how it can all go wrong was the English Super League in the sport of rugby league. At the end of the 1993 season, the rugby league in England was in a parlous state. Of the 32 professional clubs, only 14 had increased attendances over the previous season, and 17 of the clubs were technically insolvent. The product was not in high demand, and if this was to be changed, innovation was called for. So in 1995, the rugby league authorities opted to form a Super League with franchised clubs, mainly the leading clubs from the old rugby league (plans to merge neighbouring clubs into one super club were thwarted by fan hostility) plus two new franchises, the London Broncos and Paris St Germain, both designed to spread the market for the game from beyond its northern heartland of some 120 years. The Super League also opted to play a summer season rather than the traditional winter one in order to secure a contract with Sky television. End-of-season play-offs involving both the Super League and lower-tier teams were instituted. Promotion and relegation were in, then out, and then reintroduced again. The project was not a success (Wilson et al. 2015). Paris St Germain was wound up in 1997 following a visa scandal with some of its Australian players. Other clubs faced severe financial problems, notably the Bradford Bulls who matched their two Super League championships with twice going into administration. The television contract brought in revenue but cut the audience some four-fifths from its regular free-to-view spot on terrestrial television: immediate money from television was preferred to potential income from the next generation of spectators. Expanded franchises brought in the Catalan Dragons in 2006 and more recently the Toronto Wolfpack without stimulating the game in either France or Canada. The Wolfpack have now been dumped by the league for the failure to meet their playing commitments due to financial difficulties. Innovations such as the 'Magic Weekend', in which all teams played a match at the same neutral venture, were an attraction to fans who fancied a break in either Manchester or Edinburgh but did nothing to halt the steady decline of average attendance from 2007: and attendance is the ultimate performance indicator in professional sport. For all its ambitions, no sport is guaranteed an audience. The reality is that rugby league, a game that I have played and actually prefer watching to rugby union, remains a minority sport.

In contrast to the rugby competition, the EPL was a runaway success (Vamplew 2017). It was founded in 1992 when the existing first division of the four-division football league split away to become an independent organisation. The future for the EPL looked much brighter than the Super League, as in 1990, UEFA had relented on its ban of English clubs (due to hooliganism) playing in the money-spinning major European competitions, and Manchester United had won the Cup Winners' trophy the following year. All the Super League clubs could look forward to was one extracurricular match, the World Club Challenge (a 1976 innovation reintroduced in 1997 and then on a regular basis each year from 2000), between the champions of England and Australia. A second major difference with the rugby experience was that, whereas the latter originated with the rugby authorities themselves, the EPL was independent of English football's ruling body. What the EPL was interested in was money, specifically that from television. Although it had negotiated with terrestrial broadcasters, they eventually opted for a satellite, subscriber-service station. In this, the EPL was no different from the Super League and Super Rugby, except that its product was more attractive.

The optimal size for any league will vary, but Noll (2003) argues that all elite leagues are probably smaller than they should be. Big cities, especially in the United States, have too few teams partly because there is a belief that a local team is a natural monopoly and that two or more teams could not be financially viable. Some cities have no major teams in some sports, yet no one has assessed how many markets could actually support a team, especially if revenue-sharing strategies were implemented. The supply of high-quality players would not be an issue, as population growth has far outstripped the expansion of elite leagues, so unless humans are exhibiting declining athletic abilities, the number who could play at the top level would not be a constrain, especially as international markets for talent can be drawn upon in many sports.

Searching for the Holy Grail

Whatever the motives of the constituent owners, leagues have to cover their costs or they collapse. Owners do not want this to happen, as there would be no trophy to challenge for or profits to be made. If they do not survive, leagues cannot look after their members. One way to avoid failure is to continue to provide an attractive product that can be sold to fans, and this lies at the heart of their desire to develop *competitive balance*: at the level of the individual game, for the duration of a season, and into the longer term of a succession of championships. The belief is that without uncertainty of outcome, fans will tire of the league product, support will fall away, and revenues will decline so that both individual clubs and the league itself become unsustainable. Hence leagues worldwide, but especially in North America, often take action to prevent teams from becoming too dominant and maintain a competitive balance within the league. Their pursuit of this holy grail has involved adopting policies to redistribute revenue between teams, to bring in draft systems to aid the poorer-performing teams, to limit player payments so that the richer teams cannot monopolise the best talent, and to restrict player mobility between clubs for the same end. It should be stressed that the aim of competitive balance might not appeal to members of individual clubs who could feel that they could maximise home attendances by winning all the time. However, within a league, they have to subsume individual to group interests and try to maximise aggregate league attendances in the interests of all clubs. Ultimately, it is in their own interest, as they need the league in which to perform.

Paradoxically, in Scotland, we have one of the most unbalanced football leagues in the world, yet one that relies more on gate-money than most other European elite leagues. Since its establishment in 1998, no club but Celtic or Rangers has won the Scottish Premiership. They also dominate attendances with some of the largest in Europe and attract five to six times the crowds of other clubs in the league. The other clubs survive because they retain the home gates when the Celtic and Rangers visit, and they get a share of broadcasting money, even though the televised matches tend to be of either the Celtic or Rangers. In an attempt to increase attendances at the end of the season, the Scottish Premiership introduced a split when after 36 games, clubs were divided into two mini-leagues consisting of the top six and bottom six clubs, respectively. The presumption was that these leagues would contain teams of comparable quality (of course ignoring the big two) and the matches would have uncertain results. A comparison of the sixth and seventh clubs, neither of whom had anything to play for, showed that the former gained an average of 24% in attendance over the latter. However, over the years, this amounted to just 1% in club revenue, scarcely a deal-breaker (Reilly and Witt 2021).

Most studies of competitive balance have focused on team sports, possibly because creating uncertainty of outcome in individual sports is nigh to impossible.

Golf operates a handicap system but only at the grassroots level; tennis keeps seeded players apart till the later stages of a tournament; elite track and field exists as a meritocracy. In sports where gambling is significant, such as professional sprinting and horse racing, handicapping can still be applied, but in other sports, any handicapping tends to be notional, applied by the bookmakers not the promoters.

Revenue Sharing, Salary Caps, and the Draft

The type of redistribution scheme is of paramount importance. It has usually involved some sharing of gate revenue but sometimes also, both in the United States and Britain, broadcasting income. When broadcasting revenue is taken into account, total revenue sharing in the EPL was 33%, but 50% in MLB and 67% in the NFL (Sloane 2015). It has been an article of faith among economists that such revenue transfers will help create competitive balance by allowing weaker teams (or weaker-drawing teams) to strengthen their squads. However, Szymanski and Késenne (2004) have – with what they term 'reasonable assumptions', though others might disagree – demonstrated theoretically that revenue redistribution could actually widen the playing disparity between teams. I must confess that the logic behind this is not clear to me.

In Europe, most football leagues distribute broadcasting revenues to all clubs but with some reward for merit as demonstrated by league position. The most equal distribution has been in the relatively minor leagues of Austria, Bulgaria, and Switzerland. At the other end of the equality spectrum was Spain, where, until 2016/2017, clubs negotiated their own deals, which allowed Real Madrid and Barcelona to dominate the market and led to a highly polarised distribution. The EPL has been more equal than the other big European leagues and shares 50% between the clubs, allocates another 25% according to league position, and the final 25% is distributed on the basis of how many of a team's matches were televised (Wilson et al. 2018).

Many sports leagues worldwide have implemented salary caps, including, in Europe, the Rugby Union Premiership and the Super League; in Australia, the National Rugby League and the Australian Football League; and in North America, the NBA, the NHL, and the NFL. They have the dual objective of trying to improve the competitiveness of the league concerned by preventing the richer clubs from outbidding the others for the services of players, while simultaneously reducing the wage bill of clubs by limiting the auction for players (Howarth and Robinson 2008).

Salary caps are generally placed on the club rather than the player. A limit on the salary that can be paid to any player – as with the maximum wage in English soccer which lasted from 1901 to 1961 – can make for greater competitive equality between teams, as it prevents the richer clubs from attracting all the better players by offering them higher wages. Salary caps do this less well, as they generally allow clubs to spend up to a specified proportion of their revenue on overall player wages. Although the percentage is the same for all clubs, this still gives leeway for higher aggregate spending by the wealthier clubs. Some organisations have introduced 'soft' salary caps which cover off-field spending, generally dominated by coaching salaries.

In Britain, premiership rugby introduced a salary cap in 1999, which evolved into a restriction on aggregate salary spending by clubs, though (to my mind) a mistake was made in allowing two 'marquee' signings per club to be ignored in the salary total and, less of an error, additional money being allowed for long-term injury replacement and player absence on international duty. No wonder the caps failed to prevent a rise in player wages. In 2013/2014, only 5 premiership players earned over £300,000, but within 6 seasons, the figure reached almost 100. In 2019, the cap was set at £6.4 million, but this has been reduced to £5 million, and from 2022, only one 'marquee' player will be exempt from the total.

Of course, these regulations can only be effective if they are policed and enforced. Where malfeasance has been shown, three types of penalties can be imposed.

- First, there are fines, but, unless these are substantial, clubs can absorb them as an operating cost.
- More significant is the deduction of league points which can negate successful playing performance.
- Most draconian is some form of suspension, as with the banning of Manchester City from European football competitions for disregarding the FFP regulations, a decision now rescinded.

But let us not forget that the greater the impact of the penalty imposed, the greater the likelihood it will be challenged either in the domestic law courts or at the Court for Arbitration in Sport based in Lausanne. No matter what restrictions are brought in, there will be clubs that will calculate that it is worth breaking them in order to secure a championship.

Sass (2016) has developed a theoretical exposition revealing a potential weakness in the FFP policy, originally instituted in 2009 supposedly to force clubs to live within their means from normal operations. His reasoning is that, if attendances are influenced by immediate past success, without intervention to allow some over-spending by less-successful clubs, there will be a cumulative rise in support and market size of a few clubs, a likely continued on-field success by those clubs, and a systematic eroding of any competitive balance that had existed. However, this view presumes that fan support is the only major determinant of club revenue and discounts any manipulation of a club's accounts to disguise revenue sources.

Finally, we have the reverse order, which I see as North America's nod to socialism. Although it brings excitement to the pre-season, in reality, drafting is a highly imperfect exercise in prediction. A major problem with using the reverse-order draft as a quality control measure is the ability of the clubs to identify talent. A study of the NBA from 1997 to 2002 (Groothuis et al. 2009) shows that although most superstars are identified early in the draft rounds, too many high picks never feature as top players in the NBA efficiency index, a measure based on performance in all aspects of the game. Whether this was random between clubs has not been investigated. Motomura et al. (2016) examined the NBA from 1994 to 2013 and claim that high draft picks do not significantly improve a team. On average, a high pick will perform better than later ones, but there is much variance. A more important factor is the ability of a team's general manager to identify talent.

If *competitive balance* and *uncertainty of outcome* are becoming less important, as suggested in Chapter 7, then the cynic in me notes that many of the policies designed to achieve them also act to transfer income from the players to the owners. So, even if they are being paid millions, the players are still being ripped off. The introduction of rookie scales into the NBA cut first-round draft salaries by half, and if a team exercised a fourth-year option on a player, it gained 34% of its *marginal revenue product* (remember in Chapter 5; Motomura et al. 2016). Salary caps supposedly work to prevent the richest clubs from outbidding the others for the services of the most talented players, but simultaneously, they could act to control costs and aid long-term financial sustainability by reducing player ability to earn their full *economic rents* (in other words reducing player *economic welfare*).

A Note on the European Super League

The recently aborted European Super League (ESL) proposal was a natural development of capitalism at work. Capitalist organisations cannot stand still but feel that innovation is necessary for survival (and more) in a competitive economic environment. For those who view football purely as a revenue generator, there is a perennial need for constant expansion: more games and more money. The specific proposal stemmed from economic, cultural, and political tensions within European football.

The financial difficulties for elite football clubs emanating from COVID-19 restrictions provided a catalyst for some of those clubs (or rather their owners) that wished to adopt a modified version of an American franchise league. The intention was to guarantee a ESL place in perpetuity to the founding members (some of whom were not playing well enough to qualify for the forthcoming Champions League!). However, to avoid the ESL being declared a cartel (illegal in European business), five places were to be left open for competition each season. The security of financial stability which the ESL offered would make financial planning easier, and short-term debt problems would be solved by a share of the £3 billion to be advanced by financier J.P. Morgan, which was underwriting the venture. The product was to be changed. High-quality matches featuring the best teams were to be the order of the day, and match days were to be consumer experiences, though the target market was not the so-called legacy fans who attend matches but television audiences, particularly in Asia. The teams selected to join the ESL were not necessarily the best in Europe, but they had drawing power.

Notwithstanding the participation of Spanish membership clubs Real Madrid and Barcelona in the scheme, the project also stemmed from a clash of American and European sporting cultures, the former pushing profit and closed leagues, the latter seeking trophies and advocating meritocracy. Those European clubs involved were a combination of those with profit-oriented American owners and those that were utility-maximising but looking for increased revenues to back their ambitions.

For years, the wealthiest clubs in Europe had threatened a breakaway to secure concessions from UEFA, which runs the Champions League. Just before the ESL was formally announced. UEFA had conceded an expanded tournament with more places for the major European clubs and more matches to be played. The struggle to control elite European football is not over. The putative ESL clubs believe that they can offer a better product than the sometimes mismatches of the Champions League and could secure more lucrative television contracts.

References

Von Allmen, Peter (2001), 'Is the Reward System in NASCAR Efficient?', *Journal of Sports Economics* 2.1, 62–79.

Dagaev, Dmitry and Konstantin Sonin (2018), 'Winning by Losing: Incentive Incompatibility in Multiple Qualifiers', *Journal of Sports Economics* 19.8, 1122–1146.

Dolles, Harald and Sten Söderman (2005/2006), 'Implementing a Professional Football League in Japan: Challenges to Research in International Business', *Deutsches Institut Für Japanstudien* (Working Paper).

Flynn, Michael A. and Richard J. Gilbert (2001), 'The Analysis of Professional Team Sports Leagues as Joint Ventures', *Economic Journal* 111, F27–F46.

Groothuis, Peter A., James Richard Hill and Timothy Perri (2009), 'The Dilemma of Choosing Talent: Michael Jordans Are Hard to Find', *Applied Economics* 41, 3193–3198.

Howarth, Andrew and Robinson, T.A. (2008), 'The Impact of the Salary Cap in the European Rugby Super League', *International Journal of Business and Management* 3.6, 3–7.

Motomura, Akira, Kelsey V. Roberts, Daniel M Leeds and Michael A. Leeds (2016), 'Does It Pay to Build through the Draft in the National Basketball Association?', *Journal of Sports Economics* 17.5, 501–516.

Noll, Roger G. (2003), 'The Organization of Sports Leagues', *Oxford Review of Economic Policy* 19.4, 530–551.

Preston, Ian and Stefan Szymanski (2003), 'Cheating in Contests', *Oxford Review of Economic Policy* 19.4, 612–624.

Reilly, Barry and Robert Witt (2021), 'The Effect of League Design on Spectator Attendance: A Regression Discontinuity Design Analysis', *Journal of Sports Economics* 22.5, 514–545.

Sass, Markus (2016), 'Glory Hunters, Sugar Daddies, and Long-Term Competitive Balance under UEFA Financial Fair Play Policy', *Journal of Sports Economics* 17.2, 148–158.

Schwartz, Jeremy T., Justin P. Issacs and Anthony M. Carilli (2007), 'To Race or to Place?: An Empirical Investigation of the Efficiency of the NASCAR Points Competition', *Journal of Sports Economics* 8.6, 633–641.

Shmanske, Stephen (2007). 'Consistency or Heroics: Skewness, Performance, and Earnings on the PGA TOUR', *Atlantic Economics Journal* 35, 463–471.

Sloane, Peter J. (2015), 'The Economics of Football Revisited', *Scottish Journal of Political Economy* 62.1, 1–7.

Szymanski, Stefan (2003), 'The Economic Design of Sporting Contests', *Journal of Economic Literature* 41.4, 1137–1187.

Szymanski, Stefan (2004), 'Is There a European Model of Sports?' in Rodney Fort and John Fizel (eds.), *International Sports Economics Comparisons* (Praeger: Westport, CT), 19–38.

Szymanski, Stefan and Stefan Késenne (2004), 'Competitive Balance and Gate Revenue Sharing in Team Sports', *Journal of Industrial Economics* 52.1, 165–177.

Vamplew, Wray (2017), 'Creating the English Premier Football League: A Brief Economic History with Some Possible Lessons for Asian Soccer', *International Journal of the History of Sport* 34.17–18, 1807–1818.

Wilson, Rob, Plumley David and Barrett David (2015), 'Staring Into the Abyss? The State of UK Rugby's Super League', *Managing Sport and Leisure* 20.6, 293–310.

Wilson, Rob, Ramchandani, Girish and Plumley, Daniel (2018), 'Parachute Payments in English Football: Softening the Landing or Distorting the Balance?', *Journal of Global Sport Management* 3.4, 351–368.

10

SPONSORSHIP, STADIUMS, AND SUBSIDIES

Sponsorship

Sponsorship is the second-largest source of income for elite sports bodies and events, headed only by broadcasting revenue. Sponsorship, of course, often goes hand in hand with television exposure. It should be stressed that sponsors are not promoting sport – they are not sports entrepreneurs – but their own products, though their money serves to assist sport at the same time. The basis of sponsorship is *exchange theory* in which the parties involved exchange resources for their mutual benefit. The sport organisation or event offers businesses increased awareness, image enhancement (an association with a healthy competitive activity), and sales opportunities. At times, I suspect corporate executives just want to mingle with sports stars, but the bottom line is whether or not sponsorship increases their sales and profits. One clear example that it did was the sponsorship by Guinness of the 1999 Rugby World Cup. A comparison of sales during the months of the tournament with the same months the previous year showed increases in sales in Great Britain (17%), Australia (20%), South Africa (24%), and France (37%) (Gratton et al. 2012).

Sponsorship can be confusing for fans. The naming rights for Super Rugby, the pan-nation club competition, were negotiated separately in each country whose clubs were involved in the tournament, so the official title of the competition varied depending on where you were. In New Zealand, naming rights holders have included sports goods retailer Rebel Sport, copying machines franchiser U-Bix, and Telecom New Zealand. In Australia, naming sponsors have been insurance firm Suncorp, Brewers Lion Nathan, and Vodaphone. Before 1999, when cigarette advertising was banned in South Africa, the competition was sponsored by Winfield and later Vodacom. In Argentina, telecommunications carrier Personal has naming rights, and in Japan, real estate developer Mitsubishi Estate acquired naming rights in 2018, though the competition had no title sponsor in Japan during the 2016 and

DOI: 10.4324/9781003128632-10

2017 seasons. Although sponsors insist that broadcasters and the media give the full title of any competition (including the sponsors' names), fans usually identify with the ongoing bit of the title, not the part that changes as sponsors go through the revolving door. What the Super League example does demonstrate is that sponsorship is neither permanent nor reliable.

This is also the experience of the end-of-season American College Football Bowls. In 1985, there were 17 of them, none of which was sponsored, but by 2012, there were 35 such events, all of them with a sponsor in their title. However, the turnover of sponsors was frequent, which suggests they did not pay off to the corporations involved. Following an examination of bowl sponsorships between 1985 and 2012, Fizel and McNeil (2017) argue that this lack of significant profitability was reflected in the stock values of sponsoring companies. These rarely showed a rise following the sponsorship announcement, suggesting that the market did not anticipate gains from the decision.

Dark Sponsorship?

A significant source of sponsorship for sport comes from gambling: the high moral ground of yesteryear (horse racing excepted) has crumbled in the face of a need/desire for revenue. Sport and gambling are ideal bedfellows: having a bet can add to the excitement of the event, and the unpredictability of sport can create a lively betting market. Gambling lay at the origins of rule formation in sports such as cricket, pugilism, and, of course, horse racing. It continues to play a role as a major sponsor of teams and competitions. In Scottish football, all three of the major trophies are sponsored by bookmakers, and three of the SPL clubs have betting firms as their main sponsors. Several gambling companies employ sports stars as their public face, and the advertising of gambling products dominates the commercial breaks of televised sport. Less publicised is the money that comes from the national lottery that is distributed to grassroots sport around the nation, though it also puts money into major projects, such as stadium development at Hampden Park, the Millennium Stadium in Cardiff, and the new Wembley.

A major issue is whether sponsorship by alcohol and gambling businesses is an appropriate one for sport to pursue. The downside to the involvement of gambling and alcohol in sport is twofold. One is that they can lead to misbehaviour and corruption, undermining the positive contribution to the funding of sport. The other is that the advertising of these dark products can adversely affect those too susceptible to their influence, leading to a grim compulsion to participate. In effect, it is a cost-benefit decision by sports teams, though with the benefit going to them and the costs being born by other parties. Admittedly, such advertising now carries a 'health' warning, and the brewers and bookies have established charities to aid the addicted, but this is a tax-deductible expense. Tobacco sponsorship has already been outlawed because of its addictive, non-healthy nature, and it is likely that the banning of alcohol and gambling sponsorship will follow. Betting sponsors will be banned in La Liga from the start of the 2021/2022 season. The Spanish government made the decision after studies revealed that there has been a surge in young people gambling in the country, which was blamed on the sheer volume of betting companies sponsoring club kits. Almost half the league will have to chase new sponsors, as well as La Liga itself, which had an official partnership with a gambling company. However, in the United States, the relaxation of gambling laws has encouraged sports entities to search for the gambling dollar. The PGA Tour, for instance, has recognised the potential to tap into millions of dollars of extra revenue and has put betting at the heart of its product with the official leader boards carrying live odds for bets on the tournaments. One last point is that gambling need not involve sport. Indeed, an unforeseen consequence of the expansion of legalised gaming in the United States has been the scheduling for demolition of the famed Arlington racetrack. The owners of the track are making more money from owning casinos (with a guaranteed percentage of turnover coming their way) than from racing.

Stadiums and Subsidies

In the 25 years from 1990, nearly 80 premier-level stadiums were built or extensively upgraded in the United States, with some 70% of the funding coming from public coffers, usually by bond issues which were paid off via local sales and entertainment taxes (Rockerbie and Easton 2019). Specifically, the costs in 2001 dollars were as follows:

- MLB: 21 stadiums at an average cost of $533.5 million
- NHL: 23 arenas at $358.3 million
- NBA: 21 arenas at $379.5 million
- NFL: 12 stadiums at $534.4 million

Similar but less commonplace examples can be found elsewhere. The Stade de France, the national stadium built in Paris in the 1990s, had half its construction costs paid by French taxpayers, though profits went to the venue's private operators. In Australia, sports stadiums have often been owned by local authorities who leased them to Australian Rules football teams in the winter and cricket clubs in the summer (Wilson and Pomfret 2009).

In the United States, the implication is that over the years, there has been a huge (not a good word for economists to use, as it is subjective, but you know what I mean) subsidy to the team owners, many of whom are among the richest men in America. A question that must be posed is why don't the clubs themselves or private enterprises more generally bite the financial bullet? Professional sports clubs accounts are often gold medallists in opaqueness, but clubs do have money, though they often prefer to spend it on other inputs, such as players, coaching staff, and administrators rather than on the stadium itself. Put simply, if local authorities can be persuaded to foot the bill, or most of it, for a new stadium that is a rational economic decision by either profit- or utility-maximising sports bodies: owners aren't going to turn down free money. There is evidence that the subsidies are often used to create a more opulent facility than might have been necessary to attract spectators. Subsidies reduce the private marginal cost of facility amenities to teams: in other words, spending other people's money is easier than spending your own. Looking at 105 stadiums across five major American sports leagues, Propheter (2017) estimates that of every $1 million of subsidy, between $188,490 and $501,420 went on unnecessary spending. His figures are rather precise given that his methodology was to compare costs per acre for the stadium sites against those for other buildings in the area. As for private enterprise, it is simply a matter of what rate of return could be obtained in investment, especially when not all the benefits accrue to the investors. What sort of *free-riding* might occur? Even if private ventures might be more efficient, the sad story of poor returns on public investment (as outlined next) suggests that stadiums may not be a sound investment choice.

Unlike most conventional businesses that have to pay local authorities for the right to run a business, sports franchises in the United States often exert pressure on local and regional governments to have a stadium built for their use and for other operations to be subsidised. Remember franchises are mobile in the United States and are not location-specific. There is a willingness to do this by the local authorities to gain status as a 'Big League' city (city branding) and, more debatably, because of the assumed positive economic impact of having a major sports team in the community. The argument used to justify such largesse at taxpayers' expense is that the construction and operation will provide a fillip to the local economy.

The measuring tool for this is called the *multiplier*, which is the proportionate increase in overall spending generated by an initial rise in income. Imagine a football fan who wins £1,000 on the lottery and might spend some of it on club merchandise and more on celebrating his good luck in a local hostelry. The former will contribute to the wages of the shop assistant and the latter to the income of bar staff and brewery workers. In turn, their spending will contribute to the income of others: the initial spending will have stimulated the local economy to a level more than the spending itself. Contrast this with a banker who gets an unearned bonus of £1 million, but, well-knowing that he cannot trust banks, hides it under the bed, thus generating no additional spending and no multiplier effect. Returning to our football fan, not all of the lottery wins will generate income and employment in the local economy: there will be leakages to the overseas suppliers of club shirts, profit to non-local brewery shareholders, and, of course, our fan might opt to save some of his winnings or buy more tickets in the national lottery. Thus there is a limit to the local impact of the initial spending which sets the final figure on the multiplier. The argument for public subsidies is that the multiplier effect caused by firms (that benefit from the stadium and the local spending of the club) investing in new production facilities themselves and employing more local labour will outstrip the direct cost of the subsidy.

And Yet

There is no evidence that local authority investment in elite sports stadiums has yielded a net positive return. Some studies compare the economic position of a city before and after the attraction of a major team; others prefer, with due allowance for diverse local conditions, to compare cities with and without such stadiums, arenas, or teams. Whatever the method, none of them find any significant relationship between facility construction (and operation) and economic development of a city or region. Siegfried and Zimbalist (2006) suggest several reasons to account for this.

- First, individual sports teams are relatively small businesses, typically employing a small number of people, most of them (with the obvious exception of the players) unskilled part-timers on low wages.
- Then there is the *substitution* effect in that, with the great majority of attendees being local, spending on watching sport is not spent on other commodities in the area: in other words, the coming of a sports team rearranges urban spending rather than adding much to it.
- Third, much of the teams' revenues go to owners and players, a large proportion of which leaks out of the local economy in taxes, savings, and spending in the localities where they live (not usually local). These *leakages* reduce the multiplier effect of any new spending.
- Finally, there is the *budgetary gap* caused by the diversion of public funds to the sporting project. This has to be met either by increases in taxation or a reduction in public services.
- I would add a fifth factor: the relative lack of use of these facilities.

If direct economic impact is weak, there is always a possible demonstration effect of the host city receiving favourable publicity from being shown on national television. This, it is argued, could boost tourism or encourage business relocation. Neither of these holds up empirically; in particular, businesses move for a suitable labour force, a low-cost location for inputs and distribution, and a solid infrastructure (which does not include a local stadium!).

A little-studied effect is the impact that a new stadium has on existing businesses, though Propheter (2020) shows that in Sacramento, California, retail establishments within half a mile of the new Golden Center had survival times 53% shorter than similar establishments further away: but this is just one stadium in one city. However, recently, Agha and Rascher (2021) have drawn on data from 871 US metropolitan (at least one urbanised area of 50,000 or more inhabitants) and micropolitan (an urban cluster with a population of at least 10,000 but fewer than 50,000 people) areas between 2004 and 2012 to determine whether team exit and entry and the construction of new stadiums had an effect on the net number of business establishments in any of the areas. The basic source was the Census Bureau's Statistics of US Businesses. They examined 11 leagues, 65 team entries, 67 team exits, and 68 new stadiums but found few results significantly different from zero. In fact, the only positive effects were for a few minor league team entries in small markets, and these were limited to the period of stadium construction.

Stadium upgrading via subsidies can contribute to team profit (or team strengthening) by attracting extra spectators through better amenities, such as improved sightlines, more comfortable seating, high-quality catering, and large replay screens. Rockerbie and Easton (2019) examine this in detail and find that a new stadium can increase paying customers but that the evidence was mixed across sports and venues. Whether this led to improved team performance was even more unclear.

Much of the work on the economic impact of sports stadiums has been done at an aggregate level, but Tu (2005) brought a new dimension by looking at neighbourhoods in the vicinity of the FedEx Stadium, the home of the Washington Redskins (as they were then called) constructed in the late 1990s. He used hedonic pricing (remember looking at watching sport in Chapter 7), which allows numerous factors that influence house values to be assessed, such as schools, public transport, and community planning. No separate markets exist for individual housing attributes, so the value of those features cannot be directly observed and have to be estimated using statistical regression analysis (trust me: it can be done), thus allowing the influence of the stadium itself to be isolated. The construction took 30 months, so, as well as the building period itself, he also examined the 30 months before construction started and the 30 months after it was opened. His initial findings showed that properties near the stadium consistently sold at a discount compared to similar properties further away. In fact, this was the reason why the stadium was built where it was: land costs were cheaper. However, Tu then applied what is termed *difference-to-difference analysis*, which looks at the difference over time between prices of property near the stadium and compares this with differences over time of those outside the area but within the same general neighbourhood. The analysis showed that the stadium brought the greatest benefit to those properties within three miles of the stadium, but only after the stadium became operational. Clearly, the inconvenience of traffic congestion and crowd noise was offset by improved infrastructure, employment opportunities, and the use of stadium facilities. A similar exercise by Ahlfeldy and Maennig (2007) on two sports facilities constructed in Berlin in the 1990s came to a similar conclusion of positive benefits being felt up to 3,000 metres away. Feng and Humphreys (2018) looked at two stadiums in Columbus, Ohio, and found positive benefits on residential property prices within a few miles, but, as the authors themselves acknowledge, it is a major leap to go from just 9,504 property sales in 2000 to claim that overall the residents in the respective areas within a mile of the stadiums would be willing to pay $35.7 million and $222.5 million (around the downtown stadium) for the intangible benefits of living near to spectator sports facilities. If valid, such figures could bolster the case for public subsidies of stadiums. The aforementioned research deals with the impact of a new stadium via the capitalisation into residential land values, as people opt to live nearer to than farther away from the venue. But what about business land values? Propheter (2019) has undertaken a case study of the Barclays Center in Downtown Brooklyn, New York, and found a positive and distance-decaying effect with rental income per square foot falling by 3.7% for every 1,000 feet away from the arena. Whether this implies that landlords are creaming off profits from businesses that are located near the stadium is yet to be ascertained.

More research at this granular level might identify specific instances of local business impact. We have two studies relating to Charlotte, North Carolina, one on a restaurant, the other on hotels (Depken and Frank Stephenson 2018; Depken and Fore 2020), which yielded mixed results, though no overwhelmingly positive effects. An understanding of the net impact of various sporting events on local business revenues over a season or longer would be a valuable contribution to the debate on public subsidies for stadiums. However, it would be an immense research effort and might still be ignored by politicians and stadium lobby interests. They would also probably ignore (my cynical subjective judgement) the negative aspects of hosting regular sporting events, such as the rise in crime that accompanies the gathering of large numbers of people. An examination of 23 seasons and 1,773 days of MLB in St Louis showed that, after adjusting for the size of crowds and length of games (note that American baseball does not allow tied games, so the teams have to continue until there is a winner), larceny, automobile theft, minor assaults, disorderly conduct, and destruction of property all increased on game days, especially around the immediate stadium (Mares and Blackburn 2019). Typically, the aggregate increase was around 15%, with an estimated annual cost of about $1 million a year. To be fair, the crime costs of games for some major sports may be trivial relative to total citywide crime costs. NFL games in Baltimore were associated with $86,000 of crime per match (of which there were just eight a season), whereas the cost of crime in Baltimore overall was $1.2 billion a year (Kalist and Lee 2016).

There is a glimmer of hope for those proponents of 'sport puts a city on the tourist map' ideology. Caprettini (2021) suggests that a city hosting an elite soccer team, one good enough to qualify for the UEFA Champions League, could see a rise of 5%–8% in airport arrivals from cities drawn in the same group. They could anticipate this for up to three months after the actual fixture, but thereafter diminishing returns set in.

Economic Welfare Issues

Another argument is that supporting a local sports franchise will improve the quality of life in the community. This revolves around three economic concepts.

- There will be a *consumer surplus* to the match-goers if the subsidy to the team results in lower ticket prices being charged to the fans, given that the stadium costs do not have to be built into the pricing structure (Miller 2009).
- Then there are the *externalities* when consumers benefit from an activity that they do not actually purchase, as with the feel-good factor around a community when the local team wins (even for those who did not attend the game). Here I would offer a caveat. Anecdotal evidence about productivity increasing in the local economy after a team won cannot be substantiated. Any calculations are bedevilled by unsurmountable problems such as defining the geographical locality to be affected, determining whether a team was 'important' enough for beneficial externalities to ensue, and the difficulties of measuring short-term productivity changes. Of course, this says nothing about the reverse situation when the local team loses. Moreover, outside the United States, cities

often host more than one team in the same competition, so any uplift in fan mood might not be universal. I write this as a Hibernian follower who married into a Hearts-supporting family.

- Associated with externalities is a third factor, that of sport being a *public good*. You may recall that this infers that one person's consumption does not diminish another's ability to consume it. Unless a stadium is full to capacity, this is likely to be the case, and in fact, the experience might be synergistic, as one person's enjoyment might be enhanced by others also enjoying the game. Alternatively, and the more general use of the concept, is that it is non-exclusive, in that people cannot be excluded from it or charged for using it.

Measuring the values of consumer surplus, externalities, and public goods is difficult, as they are not recorded as market transactions. Economists have begun to develop ways to do this, but so far, the jury is out. However, the verdict has been returned on direct economic benefits: don't expect them. Whether any of this could be mitigated by externalities stemming from hosting a winning team is unproven.

Why Does the Charade Continue?

One can only wonder why the argument that attracting a team will promote economic development continues to be trotted out. Siegfried and Zimbalist (2006) noted that those seeking backing for their project promote the best possible scenario, too often based on false assumptions about the local value added, looking at aggregate rather than just new spending, and using unrealistic multipliers. They rarely consider negative externalities, such as crowd control problems, congestion, noise pollution, and adverse environmental footprints. These promotional impact studies sway local politicians who either want to bask in major league status at the taxpayers' expense or, if aware of historical precedent, believe that this time it will be different. Wilson and Pomfret (2009) speculate that politicians believe that sports fans will vote for those who bring them a new stadium, whereas taxpayers uninterested in sport might consider more than a single issue when casting their votes.

The Future?

As I write, two new stadium construction projects are underway. In New Zealand, plans to build a new 30,000-seat sports stadium in the earthquake-damaged city of Christchurch were given a boost after the New Zealand government approved NZ$220 million in funding from the Christchurch Regeneration Acceleration Fund for the project. The remaining NZ$253 million was to come from the city council. The stadium's capacity would be expandable to 36,000 for concerts with a standing arena. Although an anchor project in the post-earthquake rebuild, the estimated costs exceed projected benefits by NZ$70 million over 30 years and with stadium maintenance will add NZ$80 annually to every household rates bill. The hope is that more tourists will be attracted to sporting and other events than is currently envisaged. I wonder if they thought about a smaller New Zealand city that over-reached itself. Dunedin, with a population of 125,000, opted to build a 25,000-capacity stadium to host matches in the 2011 Rugby World Cup. The estimated cost was NZ$188 million, but this soared to NZ$224 million, but worse for the Dunedin ratepayers, only NZ$0.7 million of the promised NZ$45.5 million private investment eventuated. There was also an additional NZ$10 million to relocate a highway. Operating costs were continually in the red, and there were no accompanying entertainment and shopping facilities to lessen the burden, as the stadium complex was too small scale to encompass them. Consequently, several community projects had to be deferred or abandoned (Sam and Scherer 2019). In Christchurch, the council faced up to reality and opted to scale back the project, especially in view of the All Blacks demanding too high an 'incentive payment' to play matches there. However, ratepayers have now pressurised the council to revise the capacity up again. Turkeys voting for Christmas comes to mind.

However, the most recent, and by far the most expensive, stadium to be built in America runs counter to this generalisation about public subsidies. To give it its official title (though it is generally known as the SoFi Stadium), the Los Angeles Stadium and Entertainment District at Hollywood Park is estimated to cost over $5 billion, all of it private money. Investors have been attracted by plans to make it more than a stand-alone building to be used only for 20 NFL home games a year. In itself, this is double the normal amount, as the stadium will host both the LA Rams (relocated from St Louis in 2016) and the LA Chargers (relocated from San Diego in 2017). The project includes a 70,240-seat stadium and a 6,000-seat performance centre under the one roof and will anchor a 298-acre complex of office buildings, shops, restaurants, residential units, hotels, and parks. Given its proximity to the airport, the stadium has had to be sunk 100 feet down to comply with aviation height limits for buildings. In essence, the economic argument is that stadiums cannot exist as stand-alone constructions used for a few sports matches a year but should instead be flexible, multi-purpose facilities embedded in commercial developments that can attract events and customers all year round. We await the results of this venture to see if it will act as a model for future stadium construction.

References

Agha, Nola and Daniel Rascher (2021), 'Economic Development Effects of Major and Minor League Teams and Stadiums', *Journal of Sports Economics* 22.3, 274–294.

Ahlfeldy, Gabriel M. and Wolfgang Maennig (2007), 'The Impact of Sports Venues on Land Values: Evidence From Berlin', *Hamburg Contemporary Economics Discussion No. 3*, University of Hamburg.

Caprettini, Bruno (2021), 'Team Visibility and City Travel: Evidence From the UEFA Champions League Random Draw', *Journal of Sports Economics* 22.1, 85–114.

Depken, Craig A. and Benjamin L. Fore (2020), 'Firm-Level Economic Activity Before, During and After Local Events: A Case Study', *Journal of Sports Economics* 21.4, 327–334.

Depken, Craig A. and E. Frank Stephenson (2018), 'Hotel Demand Before, During, and After Sports Events. Evidence from Charlotte, North Carolina', *Economic Inquiry* 56.3, 1764–1776.

Feng, Xia and Brad Humphreys (2018), 'Assessing the Economic Impact of Sports Facilities on Residential Property Values: A Spatial Hedonic Approach', *Journal of Sports Economics* 19.2, 188–210.

Fizel, John and Chris R. McNeil (2017), 'Bowling for Dollars: Title Sponsorship of College Football Bowls', *Journal of Sports Economics* 18.2, 162–181.

Gratton, Chris, Dongfeng Liu, Girish Ramchandani and Darryl Wilson (2012), *The Global Economics of Sport* (Routledge: Abingdon).

Kalist David E. and Daniel Y. Lee (2016), 'The National Football League: Does Crime Increase on Game Day?', *Journal of Sports Economics* 17.8, 863–882.

Mares, Dennis and Emily Blackburn (2019), 'Major League Baseball and Crime: Opportunity, Spatial Patterns and Team Rivalry at St Louis Cardinal Games', *Journal of Sports Economics* 20.7, 875–902.

Miller, Phillip (2009), 'Subsidized Monopolists and Product Prices: The Case of Major League Baseball', *Applied Economics* 41, 3249–3255.

Propheter, Geoffrey (2017), 'Subsidies and Stadium Opulence', *Journal of Sports Economics* 18.1, 3–18.

Propheter, Geoffrey (2019), 'Estimating the Effect of Sports Facilities on Local Area Commercial Rents: Evidence from Brooklyn's Barclays Center', *Journal of Sports Economics* 20.1, 91–114.

Propheter, Geoffrey (2020), 'Does Proximity to a New Sports Facility Affect Existing Businesses' Survival Time?', *Journal of Sports Economics* 21.5, 451–476.

Rockerbie, Duane W. and Stephen T. Easton (2019), 'Of Bricks and Bats: New Stadiums, Talent Supply and Team Performance in Major League Baseball', *Journal of Sports Economics* 20.1, 3–24.

Sam, Michael P. and Jay Scherer (2019), 'Big Stadium, Small City: A Catalyst for Turbulence and Governance Reforms', *Urban Policy and Research* 37.3, 310–323.

Siegfried, John and Andrew Zimbalist (2006), 'The Economic Impact of Sports Facilities, Teams and Mega-Events', *Australian Economic Review* 39.4, 420–427.

Tu, Charles C. (2005), 'How Does a New Sports Stadium Affect Housing Values? The Case of FedEx Field', *Land Economics* 81.3, 379–395.

Wilson, John K. and Richard Pomfret (2009), 'Government Subsidies for Professional Sports Teams in Australia', *Australian Economic Review* 42.3, 264–275.

11
THE ECONOMICS OF SPORT MEGA-EVENTS

Problems of Definition

The definition of a sporting mega-event is subjective. For a discussion based on economic aspects, see Maennig and Zimbalist (2012b). They argue that most people would say that it had to be big in terms of budget and attendance (especially the television audience), as well as having an international element. Yet two undoubted mega-events (well they are to me) are the Super Bowl and the Tour de France, which are essentially domestic sports contests, especially the former in which all the competitors are likely to be American. However, the definition of what is 'big' is to some extent a personal opinion. Everyone would accept the Olympics and the FIFA World Cup as standouts in the category, but after that debate ensues.

Bidding and the Winner's Curse

A common feature of many mega-events is that a sports organisation owns the property rights to the event and allocates hosting rights so that no nation can unilaterally decide to hold its own world championships. In economic terms, a mega sporting event can be considered a scarce resource that is allocated to one among a group of competing potential hosts. Given the enormity and complexity of mega-events, they are not usually sold at a fixed price (like most consumer goods) nor put to a direct auction (or even a sealed one). Here we turn to *mechanism design theory*, a branch of economics focusing on allocation processes. The optimum allocation process should be geared to a specific objective, in this case the successful delivery of the mega-event (possibly, as can be seen in the following discussion, also in some instances with the extraction of maximum *economic rents*). Despite their *monopolistic* position, the rights holders have to bear in mind that the event has to be held and that a commitment to this has to be made several years before it takes place. Hence,

DOI: 10.4324/9781003128632-11

for example, both the International Olympic Committee (IOC) and FIFA opt for a two-stage process. The first brings together all applicants so that a screening process can weed out the less reliable candidates. Those left on the shortlist then provide detailed documentation of how they would run the event. They would have had the benefit of seeing their competitors' initial presentations, which could influence how they proceed in the second stage. This, unlike any auction system, is seen as a way of finding those who would both be willing to pay for, and create, a high-quality mega-event. One issue that pervades this approach is the moral hazard of *information asymmetry* (remember in Chapter 5) in which no candidate knows everything about the others and the rights owner does not know the 'true' position of any of the candidates (Humphreys and van Egteren 2012).

The potential hosts are not bidding a price – as they might in a blind auction – but seeking to persuade the rights holders that they can produce a high-quality spectacle and have the means to pay for the production. The IOC and FIFA are not concerned with the costs (they don't pay them) except in the sense that they affect the possibility of a surplus (to which they would lay a claim), so the quality of the event (however determined) is a major factor in their allocation decisions. The more grandiose the better seems to be the refrain emanating from recent decisions. To try and gain selection, the bidders attempt to outshine their rivals but simultaneously underestimate their costs. What happens is a connivance between the rights allocators (say the IOC) and the candidate cities, where the latter propose extravagant schemes (which the IOC want) but deliberately underestimate the costs. London's successful bid for 2012 ignored value-added tax, the inclusion of the Paralympics, and much of the security costs (the IOC turned a blind eye to this), which led to a rise in costs from an estimated £2.4 billion in 2005 to an estimated £9.4 billion in 2008, a steep increase, even allowing for inflation. The over-lavish spending is often 'forced on' the organisers by the rights holders exploiting their position as the sole seller of an event for which seller buyers are competing. The main cost inflator has not been operating costs but the capital expenditure on venues and infrastructure. The bidders try to balance outward extravagance with the appearance of reasonable cost. Everyone knows that the estimates are erroneous, but nobody knows by how much.

The mechanism of selection has led to what has become known by economists as the *winner's curse*, where the winner is likely to have overpaid for the rights. The problem is not so much what has been promised to be delivered but the underestimation of the costs that will be incurred and an overestimation of the benefits to be received. The likelihood of a winner's curse increases with the number of bidders, as it increases the probability that one participant will have overestimated the value of the item being auctioned. For the inhabitants of Grenoble and Montreal, it was also a taxpayer's curse, as they did not finish paying for their Olympics until 24 years and 30 years, respectively, after they were held. This contrasts with Los Angeles in 1984 where, after the financial debacle of Montreal, there were no rival bidders, and the IOC had to concede to Los Angeles's decision to use existing venues and lots of volunteers: it made a surplus of $222 million! Unfortunately for local taxpayers, the experience of a single bidder has never been repeated.

Unless they are willing to incur a loss, winning bidders must believe that the expected value will exceed the expected cost. So, too, do they accept the picture painted by their consultants, or is something else at work? Low-cost estimates could be a device to tempt governments whose underwriting of, and expenditure on, the event has to be sought. What has also to be borne in mind – and is often ignored by economic analysts – is that individuals on the selection panel and individuals on the bid teams may have their own personal agendas outside the economic costs and benefits. We are aware that some of those on the voting panels have been corrupted by promises of money and favours, but those on the bidding teams might be susceptible to visions of grandeur and celebrity, lobbying by those who stand to gain favourable press publicity, hubris, and vanity (de Nooij and van den Berg 2017).

What tempts the bidders in the first place? Some nations have seen hosting mega-events as part of a strategy for economic development. What used to be referred to as the BRICS economies (Brazil, Russia, India, China, and South Africa) – though the term has fallen into disuse – began to successfully bid to host major sports events in the second decade of this century. These developing nations saw this partially as a means to justify infrastructure spending but also as a way of attracting wealthy foreign tourists to kick-start a major sector in their economies. Although the consultants to South Africa's bid for the 2010 FIFA World Cup initially claimed that 483,000 visitors would be attracted, they later reduced the figure to 373,000. Even this was unduly optimistic, as was demonstrated by Peeters et al. (2014). Using country-by-country data over a ten-year period and allowing for visitors who would have come anyway but timed their trips to coincide with the football event and also for potential tourists who were deterred by the event (what economists call being *crowded out*, literally in this case), they found that the World Cup attracted around 220,000 additional visitors during the tournament period and perhaps 300,000 over the whole year. But at what cost? Stadium building alone equated to $4,400 per visitor, and this rises to $13,000 a head when all costs are included, suggesting that this was an expensive strategy for economic development.

Some see hosting a mega-event as bringing an economic fillip to their city. The location of the Super Bowl changes annually, and bidding to host the event is competitive. The NFL and its boosters have claimed that the Super Bowl brings up to a $500 million (2010 prices) economic boost to the host city, quite a windfall for such a short-term economic event. Indeed, the NFL explicitly uses the lure of the Super Bowl to entice cities to subsidise the construction of a stadium for a local NFL team. However, Matheson (2010) has surveyed all the academic studies of the impact on a city of hosting the Super Bowl, none of which show anything like a gain of $500 million to the local economy, usually coming in at around $100 million whether measuring employment, citizen income, or sales.

Let's end this section with a look at a mega-event with a difference. Every summer, millions of spectators watch the Tour de France sweep by and not one of them pays for the privilege. The Tour is run by a private company (the Amaury Sport Organisation) and, unlike the supposedly less profit-oriented IOC and FIFA, it does not leave its hosts with a legacy of debt. One reason for this is that it does not require the infrastructure of the Olympics or FIFA World Cup: there are no stadiums, athletes' villages, or media centres to be constructed. Instead, it relies on upgrades to normal roads (which later benefit local users), flower displays, and a few kilometres of safety fencing. Another reason is that it does not solicit bids from host towns to run the event past its doors but offers it for the same fee to all hosts of stage starts and finishes, a fee that is balanced between profit and goodwill. It is a mega-event on the cheap (Long 2012). Moreover, the tourist benefits of the tour are distributed throughout the nation and not focused on a few metropolitan areas like most mega-events.

Financing the Events

Providing that bidders can be attracted – currently, there seems no shortage, and you only need two for an auction – the monopoly power of the event organisers enables them to exert pressure on potential hosts to cover most of the associated costs. This exploitation of their monopoly position leads to one-sided contracts, with the host nation bearing the costs of construction and running the event. Hence the true economic beneficiaries from mega-events are FIFA (World Cup), the IOC (Olympic Games), and other sports organisations (Pomfret et al. 2009). The deal to host the Super Bowl has the NFL taking 100% of ticket revenue; owning, or controlling, all commercial operations, including television rights and licensing agreements; and demanding that the host cities arrange for an exemption from local and state taxes for any NFL transactions. For other mega-events, the hosts usually have ticket selling rights.

Although the organising committees for both the Olympics and FIFA World Cup manage their own commercial programmes to support the staging of the games, their sponsorship and supplier deals must not compete with those negotiated by the rights owners. FIFA also insists that only its own sponsors can advertise within a kilometre of the stadiums. In contrast, the Tour de France allows team sponsor logos to be added to the yellow jerseys and other coloured apparel worn by riders heading respective categories during the race. Although the Olympic Games are often criticised for their relationship with multi-national corporations, it is Coca-Cola and Nike money that allows the Games to be the mega-events that they are. Only if the sponsors start calling the shots should we get worried. There is not yet a Coca-Cola 100 metres or Nike Marathon. Moreover, the IOC can claim that the Games are the only international sporting event in which the competitors are not mobile advertisements, and there is no in-venue advertising. In the 1930s, the Tour de France devised the concept of a publicity caravan in which vehicles preceded the riders, their occupants distributing samples and goody bags to the spectators on route. By the 2010s, companies were paying between 200,000 and 500,000 euros to be part of the caravan (Mignot 2016). The caravan can take an hour to pass through ahead of the race itself, thus stretching the spectator experience from just a few minutes of cyclists flashing by.

The third, now often the major source, of mega-event finance comes from the selling of media rights, usually a prerogative retained by the owners of events. Here we find that a straightforward sealed bids system generally operates, a system that often leads to overpayment, unlike open auctions, which can lead to an undervaluation. The Super Bowl, the season-ending championship play-off, is the most significant sporting event in the United States. Always a sell-out event, it is the most-watched television programme in America. At the first Super Bowl in 1967, a 30-second television advert slot could be bought for $40,000. Fifty years later, inflation means that that sum would be worth $300,000, but it would have purchased only two seconds of commercial break time! Television contracts (boosted by competition between channels to gain the rights) now represent two-thirds of the Tour de France's revenue stream, but they have also tempted route cities and sponsors to pay more for access to a wider audience. The Tour played its part in making its product more amenable to live telecasts by shortening stages and timing them to end in the late afternoon to suit viewers. The organisers also broadened the boundaries of the Tour, and this internationalisation of crossing into more countries then influenced the invitations to teams, more and more of them featuring foreign riders, the share of which has risen to over 75%. The result: over 20 million television viewers worldwide per racing day.

Economic Effects

Economic impact statements relating to mega-events are misleadingly optimistic in that they only look at economic activity generated by the organisation of the event and highlight the best features while blurring the lesser ones (Kesenne 2012). From the economist's point of view, mega-events bring exogenous shocks to the economic markets in the host country, and these can be both negative and positive, something which *ante-post* impact studies fail to acknowledge.

The proponents of hosting always publish *economic impact statements* that show how the mega-event will benefit the relevant city or nation. These are produced by consultants with a vested interest in positivity. It has to be stressed that economic impact statements focus on economic activity that is likely to happen because of the event. They are not the same as *cost-benefit studies* which examine both the downside and upside of hosting. Hosts rarely commission evaluations of actual costs, revenues, and benefits. One that did, relating to the 2007 Rugby World Cup showed that an *ex ante* economic impact of €8 billion became an *ex post* €539 million (Andrieff 2012).

Hosting mega-events is often portrayed as generating large economic benefits, somewhat similar to the claims for building a stadium for a local sports team but on a larger scale. The benefits are seen as both private and public. The former include those directly associated with attending the event (e.g. ticket sales, broadcasting rights, and merchandising), indirectly associated with attendance (e.g. transport revenues, accommodation, sales of food and beverages), associated with preparing for the event (e.g. employment in construction), and those accruing after the event (especially the use value of the facilities and infrastructure). Usually, because not all these benefits accrue to those in the private sector who might fund the event, governments step in with large public subsidies which they justify on the grounds that the event will increase the skill base of the nation; improve the external image of the country leading to more tourism, trade, and inward investment; create greater efficiency vis better infrastructure; stimulate depressed regions; and generally promote a national feel-good factor.

Yet, as we have seen from a few of the previous examples, hosts rarely gain any substantial direct economic benefit from a mega-event. Indeed, almost all mega-events turn out to be economically disappointing for the host countries. For a plethora of evidence on this, see Maennig and Zimbalist (2012a). Those wishing to host an event always inflate its potential benefits because they want government support for the project and governments like to be assured that they are getting a decent bang for their bucks. The reality is that this rarely happens. Almost universally, academic economists (those not getting the consultancy fees) calculate that the events fail to generate financial gains for the government of the host country.

Economic arguments have focused on three main avenues: the creation of jobs, tourism, and the infrastructural legacy.

- There is the promise of employment during the construction and staging period, with the prospect of longer-term jobs if the legacy is a positive one. The former is a reasonable assumption, which could generate spending in the local economy; the latter is often an unfulfilled dream. Hagn and Maennig (2009) compared levels of unemployment in 12 venues for the 2006 FIFA World Cup with that of 63 other German cities over the period 1998–2007 and found no significant variation.
- It is hoped that marketing and media exposure associated with the event will attract tourists who will spend money in the local economy. Again, this seems reasonable, but optimism has to be tempered by an awareness of time-switchers (who would have come anyway but changed their dates to coincide with the event) and casuals (who would have come irrespective of the event). Moreover, care needs to be had in defining the size of the economy to be benefitted. For example, if London attracted visitors from elsewhere in the United Kingdom, their spending might have been a gain for the metropolis but a loss to the districts where they came from, with an overall neutral impact.
- There is the possibility of using the events as an excuse to develop transport and sporting infrastructure and kick-start urban regeneration. Both Rome and Tokyo used this strategy when they hosted the Olympics in the early 1960s. The leading question is why did they not prioritise such construction before? Moreover, there is the danger that some of the buildings could be too specific to the mega-event and not that useable later. Too often bidders, desirous to win the 'auction', promise over-lavish facilities which then cause legacy problems by being either underutilised or having to be rented out at uneconomic fees. Rarely is it ever considered that, if a city did not need the facilities before the event, why should it require them after it? Of course, if the event stimulated greater participation in sport, there may be a demand for some of the facilities, but there is no compelling evidence that this has ever occurred in more than the very short run; hence, so many white elephant buildings that lie underutilised or are demolished after the event (Kesenne 2012).

What results do we get when we do the sums? Overall, a host of economic impact studies give a thumbs down to sporting mega-events as a means of helping enrich a city or a nation. Research shows no significant increases in tourism, full-time employment, or regional economic growth.

However, if there are any positive studies, there is a possible case for the politicians and sports administrators to argue that lessons have been learned, and this time it will be different. A study of seven FIFA World Cups and nine UEFA European Championships found an average rise of about 16% in league match attendances at the host grounds in the five years after the event compared to the five years before and smaller, but still significant, rises at other league grounds (Szymanski and Drut 2020). Some of this would stem from the necessary upgrading of facilities, but publicity and a feel-good factor might also play a role. In revenue terms, this might amount to about £3 million a season for an EPL club or one from La Liga, not a major contribution to their coffers. Nevertheless, there are a few reputable academic studies which show economic positivity for hosting a sports mega-event. Two that do this use a method termed *difference to difference* in which changes in areas directly linked to the event are compared with changes in more neutral areas over a period of time on either side of the event. Jasmand and Maennig (2008) look at employment creation and income generation in regions close to venues of the 1972 Munich Summer Olympics compared to other regions in Germany in the period 1961–1988. They found that, even when structurally similar areas were compared, Olympic regions fared better in income terms, but no significant differences in employment were noted. Conversely, Hotchkiss et al. (2003), who looked at the Atlanta Games of 1996 (using data 1985–2000) found a 17% differential rise in employment (approximately 293,000 jobs) between counties near to Olympic activity and other Georgian counties but no evidence of increased wages accompanying that. Neither study allows for a statement on the overall effect of the Olympics on the host city and nations involved, as the authors acknowledge that other non-Olympic influences could have been operative. It could be – as we saw in the previous chapter – that local impacts might be the greatest effect of mega-events, though these are never stressed by the proponents. One final point: even acknowledged benefits have to have their opportunity cost considered and it has to be asked whether public funds could have been expended on other projects with a greater yield?

References

Andrieff, Wladimir (2012), 'The Winner's Curse: Why Is the Cost of Mega Sporting Events so Often Underestimated?' in Wolfgang Maennig and Andrew Zimbalist (eds.), *International Handbook on the Economics of Mega Sporting Events* (Edward Elgar: Cheltenham), 32–69.

De Nooij, Michiel and Marcel van den Berg (2017), 'The Bidding Paradox: Why Politicians Favor Hosting Mega Sports Events Despite the Bleak Economic Prospects', *Journal of Sport and Social Issues* 42.1, 68–92.

Hagn, Florian and Wolfgang Maennig (2009), 'Large Sports Events and Unemployment. The Case of the 2006 Soccer World Cup in Germany', *Applied Economics* 41, 3295–3302.

Hotchkiss, Julie L., Robert E. Moore and Stephenie M. Zobay (2003), 'Impact of the 1996 Summer Olympic Games on Employment and Wages in Georgia', *Southern Economic Journal* 69.3, 691–704.

Humphreys, Brad R. and Henry van Egteren (2012), 'Mega Sporting Event Bidding, Mechanism Design and Rent Extraction' in Wolfgang Maennig and Andrew Zimbalist (eds.), *International Handbook on the Economics of Mega Sporting Events* (Edward Elgar: Cheltenham), 17–36.

Jasmand, Stephanie and Wolfgang Maennig (2008), 'Regional Income and Employment Effects of the 1972 Munich Summer Olympic Games', *Regional Studies* 42.7, 991–1002.

Kesenne, Stefan (2012), 'The Economic Impact, Costs and Benefits of the FIFA World Cup and the Olympic Games: Who Wins, Who Loses?' in Wolfgang Maennig and Andrew Zimbalist (eds.), *International Handbook on the Economics of Mega Sporting Events* (Edward Elgar: Cheltenham), 270–278.

Long, Judith Grant (2012). 'Tour de France: A Bargain Among Sporting Mega Events?' in Wolfgang Maennig and Andrew Zimbalist (eds.), *International Handbook on the Economics of Mega Sporting Events* (Edward Elgar: Cheltenham), 357–385.

Maennig, Wolfgang and Andrew Zimbalist (eds.) (2012a), *International Handbook on the Economics of Mega Sporting Events* (Edward Elgar: Cheltenham).

Maennig, Wolfgang and Andrew Zimbalist (2012b), 'What Is a Mega Sporting Event?' in Wolfgang Maennig and Andrew Zimbalist (eds.), *International Handbook on the Economics of Mega Sporting Events* (Edward Elgar: Cheltenham), 9–14.

Matheson, Victor (2010), 'Economics of the Super Bowl', *North American Society of Sports Economists Working Paper* 1001.

Mignot, Jean-François (2016), 'An Economic History of the Tour de France, 1903–2015' in Richard Pomfret and John K. Wilson (eds.), *Sport Through the Lens of Economic History* (Edward Elgar: Cheltenham), 55–70.

Peeters, Thomas, Victor Matheson and Stefan Szymanski (2014), 'Tourism and the 2010 World Cup: Lessons for Developing Countries', *Journal of African Economies* 23.2, 290–320.

Pomfret, Richard, John Wilson and Bernhard Lobmayr (2009), 'Bidding for Sports Mega-Events', University of Adelaide, School of Economics Working Paper Series No: 0089 (2009-30).

Szymanski, Stefan and Bastien Drut (2020), 'The Private Benefit of Public Funding: The FIFA World Cup, UEFA European Championships and Attendance at Host Country League Soccer', *Journal of Sports Economics* 21.7, 723–745.

12

THE GLOBAL SPORTS ECONOMY

Trading Goods, Player Migration, and International Organisations

Globalisation

Many observers confuse globalisation with Americanisation, but the United States has not dominated sport as it has other areas of popular culture, such as film, television, and pop music. Indeed, two major American sports, American football and baseball, have failed to be taken up by sufficient nations to qualify for the Olympics, that greatest of global sports festivals. Instead, my inclination is to see globalisation as referring to the various sports markets, those for sport products and sports producers which have shifted from being domestically oriented to having a significant international dimension. Professional sports clubs operate in two main markets: that for labour, which is their major input, and that for the consumption of their output. In many sports, the market for players has become international, one in which the richest leagues and clubs attract the most talented by offering the highest salaries. This lessens the chances for start up leagues and their clubs to obtain or retain skilled players who can help deliver a quality product. Clubs in such leagues often become selling clubs which recruit players cheaply, develop their skills, and make a profit by then selling them on to a richer club. The K-League in Korea, for example, has found that the best Korean players prefer to play outside their homeland because of the higher rewards available elsewhere (Nahm 2016). The consumption of the spectator product can be both domestic and, thanks to television, international. Again using the K-League as an example, it faces a domestic challenge from baseball where league games are televised daily while soccer struggles to get one channel interested. There is also televised competition from foreign football, especially where Korean players are involved (Nahm 2016).

DOI: 10.4324/9781003128632-12

Production and Consumption

Player equipment and costumes were first produced near the point of purchase; indeed, some were probably made by the players themselves from available raw materials. As demand increased, two quality segments emerged. At the high end of the market, craft production dominated, but meeting the lower-quality demand of a mass market necessitated mass production where centralisation of output became the norm. In the latter quarter of the twentieth century, however, came a major change as Western sports goods 'producers' sought cheap, non-unionised, labourers in the developing world who worked under minimal safety and environmental regulation. The output of much sports equipment became located far from its purchase and end-use, a major change from its artisanal beginnings. Today the sports goods market is a global one dominated by an *oligopoly* of transnational producers (no prizes for naming them) with a fringe of small and medium-sized local companies in domestic markets. There are two basic groups of sports goods: *trite* ones which can be switched to other sports (especially footwear) or to non-sport purposes (leisurewear) and those that have a more *specialised* function such as tennis racquets, cricket balls, and surfboards. Obviously, the markets for the latter are smaller and more segmented than for trite goods. Desbordes et al. (2019) estimate that in value terms sports equipment comprises 40% of the market, textiles and accessories 35%, and sports shoes 25%. Competition between the dominant firms is rarely by price but by a combination of marketing strategies and product innovation. The basic marketing strategies revolve around having the product endorsed by a star performer or becoming adopted as the official supplier to a major team or event. The need to innovate has led to firms allocating over 5% of their turnover to research and development which in turn limits the life cycle of any particular sports good. Demand for sports goods is volatile partly through changes in fashion both in the style of the product and in the participation levels in particular sports (Andreff 2006a).

We do not know the extent of international trade in sports goods, as it is often subsumed into wider categories in published data or, especially in developing countries, not published at all. What we do know is that it could be larger, as many sports goods and services are still subjected to high tariffs and other measures of protectionism. Free trade enables more efficient resource allocation by exploiting the *economies of scale* from specialisation: average costs of production decrease as the production scale increases. Yet the world is not one of free trade but of free trade areas and free trade agreements with protective barriers raised against non-signatories. This is where political economy raises its head, as tariffs can be imposed to raise revenue for a government (the assumption being that there will still be a demand even with the higher price) or to protect domestic industry (where the assumption is that this will choke off demand for the external product).

Free trade agreements work to the advantage of all parties, as they allow greater overall production to occur by encouraging the benefits of specialisation and economies of scale under the banner of *comparative advantage*. Following Booth (2009), a good way to comprehend comparative advantage is to use a sporting analogy. Consider a football team, let's say Brazil in the 1970s in which the coach reckoned the great Pelé was the best forward and the best goalkeeper. He had an absolute advantage over any of his teammates in either position. The coach had to decide where his comparative advantage lay: could another player perform almost as well as Pelé in the goals or almost as well in attack? He decided that Pelé did more for Brazil in scoring goals than in preventing them. Clearly, if one country has an *absolute advantage* over another in producing one product, it would make sense to focus on that and trade it for other goods where it does not have such an advantage. However, even if that country had an absolute advantage in all goods, more overall could be produced if it concentrated on the ones where it had the greatest productive efficiency and gained economies of scale, leaving others to produce the rest and obtain their own economies of scale.

Going back to the deficiency of trade statistics, even if we had the data, we would then have to work out how much of the trade was an intra-firm transfer of products, something which has emerged as the major producers have relocated their manufacturing plants abroad where labour is plentiful, non-unionised and cheap. For example, although its headquarters are located in the United States, Nike now produces virtually nothing in America, with most of its production coming from factories located in Asia and product development, financing, marketing, governance, and sales being controlled and co-ordinated from the States. Other firms have done similarly either via subcontracting deals with local producers or by direct investment in subsidiaries in low-unit labour cost countries. What has developed is a North/South trade in sports goods, economists' shorthand for trade between developed and developing countries. Generally, developed countries have become net importers of sporting goods, and developing countries, especially in Asia, have become net exporters, themselves exploiting their own comparative advantage by specialising in certain lines. Hence bicycle tyres were a specialty of Malaysia; sports footwear, tennis balls, and tennis racquets mainly emanated from South Korea and Taiwan; and footballs from India, Thailand, and, especially, Pakistan (Andreff 2006b; Sungho and Kyoo 2018).

Whereas equipment and costume manufacture were feasible for centralised mass production, the spectator product was created at a multitude of local production points, although the *delocalisation* of spectator sport means that the consumption of spectator products has also diverged from being immediately located at the point of production to being consumed via electronic media away from the stadium or sports arena. Historically, though, team spectator sports production has always been tied to a local firm and remains the case even when the market has extended to have regional, national, or even international dimensions. Promoters of team sports still present the team as being representative of the locality. Football, baseball, and other teams have persisted as traditional firms, consisting usually of a single unit with a single owner or small group of owners with a single major product line. Notwithstanding later tendencies to import players, capital, and management, the site of production has remained localised, and although relocations, mergers, and franchise changes may have moved the site of production, it is still at a single point.

However, for elite non-team sports, the production point changes during the season as Formula 1 motor racing, the European and American golf tours, the ATP tennis circuit, and the like take their production schedules around the world, though still serving a global market as the consumer market for elite sport has become more international, thanks to television. Providing that they can afford the subscription or the drinks in the sports bar, sports consumers now get unprecedented global coverage of sport.

Professionals

The market for high-level sporting talent has also globalised with the migration of elite performers to earn their livings away from their domestic markets. Some professionals, such as Formula I drivers, are perpetually peripatetic, as the venue for their sport changes continually. Others choose to relocate residentially in search of higher wages, often moving to Europe by taking advantage of agreements made by the EU (Kolpak, Malaja, and Cotonou for instance), which allowed non-EU sportspersons to sign contracts with European sports teams if their nation had a trade agreement with the EU. In 1986, the five major European football leagues contained 9.1% of foreign players. By 2014/2015, this had risen to 46.7%. It was accentuated by the exploitation of numerous dual citizenship arrangements with former colonies. In 2015, 46% of the players who had participated in the Latin American Cup and 66% of those from the African Nations Cup belonged to European clubs. (Sánchez et al. 2019).

Brexit means that European footballers will now need a visa to work in the United Kingdom. To qualify for a Governing Body Endorsement (GBE), awarded by the Football Association, players will have to meet criteria (15 points are required) that have been agreed by the FA, the EPL, and the EFL and apply to players worldwide. Top players will still have no problem gaining entry. A player over the age of 21 from a country ranked within FIFAs top 50, who has played 70% of their country's matches over the previous 24 months will automatically get a GBE. Similarly, those playing for a club in a band 1 league (the Bundesliga, La Liga, Serie A, and Ligue 1) and appear on a team sheet just the once, get 12 points. Sit on the bench for a single Champions League group game and that is five more. However, players in lower-quality leagues who play internationals for a nation outside the FIFA top 50 will have difficulties in gaining a GBE. This could have serious consequences for some Championship teams that have built business models around acquiring talented players from obscure places. Brexit has implications for football in particular but also for less-Europeanised sports such as cricket where English counties had used the Kolpak rule to recruit overseas players who did not count as overseas in the first-class cricket regulations.

Economists have focused on two major aspects of this flow of skilled labour across national borders: the effect of the muscle drain on recipient clubs and the influence on the national teams in both the exporting and importing countries. Milanovic (2005) looked at the European Champions League, Serie A in Italy, and the World Cup and concluded that increased player migration had produced increased inequality of results among clubs but lower inequality at the national level. Building on his work, Royuela and Gásquez (2019), using more data (971 clubs from 71 leagues) and a more sophisticated analysis, maintained that those leagues with more foreign players displayed better results in world rankings, as measured by Elo ratings (named after their inventor a Hungarian American physicist, Arpad Elo). First used in chess, these ratings take account of the kind of match, whether a team was at home or away, and the goal difference in the match result. However, within individual leagues, the number of foreign players had little effect, as all participating clubs were subject to the same restrictions on recruitment: what mattered was the financial power to purchase the best foreign players. Berlinschi et al. (2013) noted that migrant sportspeople, while working in one country, are still eligible to represent their home nation in international matches: herein lies some compensation for the country that loses its best players to foreign clubs, as those players could improve their *human capital* by playing and training alongside stars elsewhere. They looked at 202 national teams and concluded that the performance of national sides improved if players left for countries with higher-ranked leagues and clubs. Domestic players at recipient clubs could also benefit from *knowledge transfer* – learning techniques and approaches from players coached in a different culture – provided that they were not crowded out by the incomers.

An examination of European basketball showed that the influx of labour tended to be from the United States but by players who would not make the American national team (Alvarez et al. 2011). A distinction was drawn between *transitory effects* (in which domestic players improved their club performance when playing alongside higher-quality foreign players) and *permanent effects* (which saw the athletes becoming better players in the longer term by having to compete harder for their place in the side and learning new skills). The latter effect was confirmed by demonstrating that countries with more imported players in their clubs achieved more in world and European championships.

Since the mid-1990s, the NBA draft has been widened to include international players who initially (up to 2002) tended to perform above expectations (as adjusted for draft position), leading clubs to look for more overseas recruits so that by 2003 international players comprised over a third of draftees. However, from then on, first-round picks from outside the United States tended to underperform relative to expectations, suggesting that clubs had overacted to the success of the first tranche. More generally, a change in the NBA draft regulations encouraged greater risk-taking in selections with greater monetary gains to be made if a selection made the grade, so some clubs took chances on players about whom they had less information than they possessed for college players (Motomura 2016).

I would add a few caveats to these studies. As with all discussions of inequality between teams, much depends on the specific measures of competitive balance that are employed; there will be a lag between cause and effect, as neither players nor teams can be developed overnight; and, as detailed in Royuela and Gásquez (2019), countries vary in the number of foreign players allowed to join a club.

Global Sports Organisations

There are three types of global sports organisations, though most, like FIFA, are international governing bodies of sport. Others, such as the IOC, are event-oriented bodies, and a third group, including the World Anti-Doping Agency, are function-related (Gratton et al. 2012). The numbers of members of these organisations reflect the globalisation of the sport. In 2001, the international organisation for volleyball had 218 nations registered; for basketball, it was 211; tennis 190; 179 in judo; and 176 in swimming. Membership in the IOC was only 7 in 1900, had risen to 46 in 1936, 130 in 1972, and 202 by 2004 (Andreff 2008).

To some observers, including myself, the commercial imperative of many governing bodies has become more important than their base objective of administrating and advancing the cause of their sports: the means to an end has become an end in itself. Although their basic role is to govern sport, they are also concerned with running world championships for which they hold a monopoly position. As the demand for broadcasting such events has risen significantly, this has enabled them to secure substantially increased revenues from either broadcasters or host nations. So important has this become that, despite COVID-19 being rampant in Japan, the recent Tokyo Olympics were not cancelled because of the IOC's need for the broadcasting revenue: crowds at the venues could be done without but not the global audience watching their screens.

FIFA, for example, has been the ruling body of football (soccer), the world's most popular sport, since 1904. FIFA exerts control or influence on everyone who participates in football from the players to the spectators, from coaches to club shareholders, from officials to sponsors. It has now transformed from being an international sporting body concerned with setting rules and promoting competition within Europe to becoming a transnational organisation pursuing, cultural, humanitarian, and development ambitions. Today, FIFA has more member countries than the United Nations and has become one of the most financially powerful international non-government organisations. It has consolidated its position by securing regulatory privileges from national governments which have restricted state intervention in such matters as anti-competitive behaviours, control of employment relations, and internal governance. The growing influence of non-European nations in the second half of the twentieth century forced FIFA to make good on its initial tenet of promoting 'the game of association football in every way it deems fit'. This has led to football development programmes being instigated across the globe. In turn, this forced FIFA into becoming a fully-fledged economic operator in order to finance these activities. It began by securing sponsorship from the likes of Nike and Adidas, moved on to merchandising, but gained its primary source of income from selling the broadcasting rights to the World Cup, a trophy it had instigated in 1930. In the period 2011–2014, its income of $5.7 billion vastly exceeded its expenses of $2.2 billion. Yet it could be argued that it is not a typical *profit-maximising, capitalist enterprise*, as its surpluses are not distributed according to the size of shareholding but to member associations either equally or according to need. Despite its entrepreneurial activity FIFA remains a member organisation, but it no longer needs the subscriptions of these members which now account for less than 1% of its income. As a consequence even relatively wealthy member associations receive more money from FIFA than they actually contribute to the organisation (Eisenberg 2006).

Adverse Economic Welfare

There are economic welfare downsides to the globalisation of sport.

Elite sportspersons operate in a global market for their services and frequently move to where the money is. However, players who migrate for a job are different from those who switch national allegiances. The right to represent a country comes from three sources:

- jus soli (territorial birth rate),
- jus sanguines (blood ties), and
- jus nexi ('genuine' connection by virtue of residence, marriage, etc.).

Blood ties explain why in the history of the FIFA World Cup there have always been between 8% and 12% foreign-born players participating in the finals (Oonk 2020). However, citizenship by connection is becoming exploited by nations desperate to recruit actual and potential sports stars to bring them international sporting success. The loss of such athletes of course means a loss of economic welfare for the domestic supporters. Additionally, any investment in the sportspersons who opt to depart has to be written off and yields no rate of return. The obvious point to make is that the direction of travel is more often than not from poorer to richer countries. Young African footballers are an example. Looking for the raised socio-economic status of playing in Europe is a career goal for many of them. A few make it, but most do not. Esson (2015) records the shame of those who were recruited legitimately by European clubs, failed to make the grade, and were too ashamed to return home. More concerning though were those 'recruited' by scam agents, their families charged for the 'opportunity', and the youths abandoned in Europe (some 7,000 of them across France in the decade from 2005).

An even worse fate has awaited some other migrant workers in the sports sector. An average of 12 workers from India, Pakistan, Nepal, Bangladesh, and Sri Lanka have died each week in Qatar since it won the right in December 2010 to host the 2022 FIFA World Cup and began an unprecedented building programme, in preparation for the football tournament, including, a new airport, roads, public transport systems, hotels, and seven new stadiums. Most of the workers who died were only in the country because Qatar was hosting the FIFA event. The Qataris claim that most deaths were from natural causes and that the number of deaths – which it does not dispute – is proportionate to the size of the migrant workforce, while FIFA itself maintained the frequency of accidents on FIFA World Cup construction sites has been low when compared to other major construction projects around the world.

The globalisation of football also adversely affects another group of workers, as the international division of labour in the production of footballs involves child employment. In the early 1990s, much of the world's output of footballs stemmed from young boys and girls hand sewing together panels of leather or synthetic materials. At the time, the industry centred on Sialkot in Pakistan. A football could sell for £50; the six-year-old Pakistani child who stitched it together got paid the equivalent of 10 pence. Even with distribution and marketing costs, and allowing for the press's gravitation to worst-case scenarios, this was a classic example of corporate capitalism exploiting market forces to its advantage. Capitalism has no moral principles where labour is plentiful and cheap: legally their primary duty is to their shareholders, not their workforce. Not until they were exposed did the multinationals see a need to change the system, and then they agreed to purchase footballs only from companies that accepted International Labour Organisation monitoring. However, the agreements were only with the major international sports goods companies and applied only to the top grade of production. Moreover, there is no credible way of identifying whether or not a football has been produced by a child. Child labour is illegal in India and Pakistan but few seem to care that the law is infringed to produce sports equipment. Not the national or state governments that simply accept the situation, not the multinational corporations that subcontract the production of their wares to middlemen in those nations, not even the Save the Children Charity which argued that stitching footballs was not as bad as other trades, and certainly not the consumers who continued to buy footballs by the millions (Nadvi et al. 2011). Even Fairtrade's endorsements of certain footballs have not dented the market share of more exploitative producers (Abbasi and Din 2020).

References

Abbasi, Javeria Younas and Muslahi Ud Din (2020), 'Fairtrade and Workers' Welfare: A Case Study of the Soccer Industry in Pakistan', *Journal of Asian and African Studies* 55.4, 536–555.

Alvarez, Jaime, David Forrest, Ismael Sanz and Juan de Dios Tena (2011), 'Impact of Importing Foreign Talent on Performance Levels of Local Co-Workers', *Labour Economics* 18, 287–296.

Andreff, Wladimir (2006a), 'The Sports Goods Industry' in Wladimir Andreff and Stefan Szymanski (eds.), *Handbook on the Economics of Sport* (Edward Elgar: Cheltenham), 27–39.

Andreff, Wladimir (2006b), 'International Trade in Sports Goods' in Wladimir Andreff and Stefan Szymanski (eds.), *Handbook of the Economics of Sport* (Edward Elgar: Cheltenham), 59–61.

Andreff, Wladimir (2008), 'Globalization of the Sports Economy', *Revista Di Diritto Ed Economia Dello Sport* 4.3, 13–32.

Berlinschi, Ruxanda, Jeroen Schokkaert and Johan Swinnen (2013), 'When Drains and Gains Coincide: Migration and International Football Performance', *Labour Economics* 21, 1–14.

Booth, Ross (2009), 'Sports Economics', *Australian Economic Review* 42.3, 377–385.

Desbordes, Michel, Pascal Aymar and Christopher Hautbois (eds.) (2019), *The Global Sports Economy: Contemporary Issues* (Routledge: Abingdon).

Eisenberg, Christiane (2006), 'FIFA 1975–2000: The Business of a Football Development Organisation', *Historical Social Research* 31.1, 55–68.

Esson, James (2015), 'Better Off at Home? Rethinking Responses to Trafficked West African Footballers in Europe', *Journal of Ethnic and Migration Studies* 41.3, 512–530.

Gratton, Chris, Dongfeng Liu, Girish Ramchandani and Darryl Wilson (2012), *The Global Economics of Sport* (Routledge: Abingdon)

Milanovic, Branko (2005), 'Globalization and Goals: Does Soccer Show the Way?', *Review of International Political Economy* 12.5, 829–850.

Motomura, Akira (2016), 'MoneyRoundball? The Drafting of International Players by National Basketball Association Teams', *Journal of Sports Economics* 17.2, 175–206.

Nadvi, Khalid, Peter Lund-Thomsen, Hong Xue and Navjote Khara (2011), 'Playing Against China: Global Value Chains and Labour Standards in the International Sports Goods Industry,' *Global Networks* 11.3, 334–354.

Nahm, Jae (2016), 'Comments on 'Professional Asian Football Leagues and the Global Market'', *Asian Economic Policy Review* 11, 41–42.

Oonk, Gijsbert (2020), 'Who May Represent the Country? Football, Citizenship, Migration and National Identity at the FIFA World Cup', *International Journal of the History of Sport* 17.11, 1046–1065.

Royuela, Vicente and Roberto Gásquez (2019), 'On the Influence of Foreign Players on the Success of Football Clubs', *Journal of Sports Economics* 20.5, 718–741.

Sánchez, Luis Carlos, Ángel Barajas and Patricio Sánchez-Fernández (2019), 'Sport Finance' in Jaume Garcia Villar (ed.), *Sport (and) Economies* (Nisan: Madrid), 327–367.

Sungho, Cho and Hong Lim Kyoo, (2018), 'International Trade in Sports Products: Free Trade Agreements, Sporting Goods and Playing Talent' in Mark Dodds, Kevin Heisey and Aila Ahonen (eds.), *Routledge Handbook of International Sport Business* (Routledge: Abingdon), 184–198.

13

MEDALS, HEALTH AND WELFARE, AND THE THIRD SECTOR

Buying Medals

Nationalistic fervour is heightened every four years by the Olympic Games, which have placed the nation at the centre of affairs. Individual competitors cannot enter but must be nominated by the Olympic Committee of their nation. National flags are hoisted, national anthems played, and medals are listed by countries in league tables. As Morton (2000) has demonstrated in the context of the Sydney Olympics, there are many ways in which medal tallies can be calculated to the best advantage of particular countries. The eastern communist bloc prefers medals in relation to GDP; lower populated nations like New Zealand and Cuba opt for a demographic ratio; large countries with vast sporting resources take numerical aggregates. Whatever the method of calculation, the lure of a medal is strong among politicians, as sporting success at the Olympics has come to represent the benefits of particular political ideologies: and the reverse. Sporting failure has caused governments to rethink their sports policies so as to restore their international image.

The relatively poor performance by Team Great Britain at the Atlanta Olympics in 1996, where there was but one gold in the haul of 15 medals, was seen by Prime Minister John Major as a comment on his government. In an attempt put the great back in Great Britain, his response was to push money into elite Olympic sports and raise the government subsidy from £5 million to £54 million, much of it spent on allowing athletes to train full time under the best coaches with state-of-the-art equipment and facilities. The result? Sydney in 2000 brought 28 medals, 11 of them gold. When the Olympics came to London in 2012, 65 medals were won at a cost of just over £4 million each!

Whether buying medals achieves any political objectives has not really been tested, but a study of international football in sub-Saharan Africa suggests that sporting success can bring some positive *externalities*. Based on over 37,000

DOI: 10.4324/9781003128632-13

respondents in 25 countries and covering 69 matches between 2002 and 2015, Depetris-Chauvin et al. (2020) found that if teams had some success, this led to a significant weakening of ethnic identity (as opposed to national identification), an improvement in attitudes towards those of other ethnicities, and a reduction in inter-ethnic violence. However, in a warning to political leaders who want to see sporting success further their popularity, there is no evidence that this raised trust in the ruling party or approval for the incumbent head of government.

More influential though has been the possibility of basking in the reflected glory from medals. History shows that home advantage has often delivered a superabundance of medals thanks to crowd support and the ability to field a large team. Australia, for example, won 85 medals at the 1952 Helsinki Games, but on home territory, at Melbourne, only four years later, the aggregate upped to 314. History almost repeated itself in 2002 at the Sydney Games where the home nation gained 630 medals, just under 50% more than at the previous Olympics in Atlanta. Yet home venue success does not always occur. Canada is the sole country to have hosted the Games without winning a solitary gold medal, and it did it twice: at Montreal in 1976 and again at the Calgary Winter Olympics in 1988. This did not stop the Canadians applying again – successfully for the Vancouver Winter Games of 2010 – but this time with an avowed (and financed to the tune of C$117 million) policy of getting back on the podium. It was little surprise that this time the Canadians topped the gold medal table.

Rewilak (2021) argues that there are only two statistically significant determinants of Olympic success: population size (larger countries will have more high-quality athletes) and, the most obvious way to guarantee a medal haul (with the notable exception of Canada in 1976 and 1988), hosting the Olympics. But is it worth the cost? In reaching for the sun, many get burned, and the toxic atmosphere created in the pursuit of winning has had deleterious effects on those subjected to the pressure. For them, sport was certainly not health-giving.

Don't Worry, Be Happy

As we have seen, most economic studies have suggested that the costs of holding mega sports events outweigh the economic benefits received. This had led to a search for less tangible benefits – community engagement, inspiring the next generation, and the 'feel-good' factor – to help balance the books. Mega-events may not enrich a host population, but could they make it happier? To answer this question, we must be able to measure happiness, but there is no real proxy measurement available: counting smiley faces in a crowd does not fit the bill. What we do have is something that has emerged over the past half-century: surveys of life satisfaction based on surveys of individuals in which they are asked something along the lines of 'how satisfied are you with your current life?' with a range of answers accepted from 'very, fairly, not very, and not at all'. There could be problems with individuals misreporting, but the size of the samples (generally of at least 1,000) renders any such misrepresentative non-systematic and unlikely to influence the overall results. Take my word for it:

this is right. Subjective well-being data is based on the concept of *experienced utility*, which many economists regard as an appropriate way to measure welfare. Most economics associated with consumer behaviour use utility (a measure of satisfaction) as something which determines choices when purchasing decisions are being made. Such decisions reveal consumer preference in the sense that consumers believe the pattern of spending they have adopted will bring them the greatest aggregate satisfaction. In essence, it is based on expectations, on hoped-for outcomes. In contrast, experienced utility measures the actual experience once choices have been made.

What then about sport and happiness? A breakthrough work here was Kavetsos and Szymanski (2010). These two economists elected, first, to find out if hosting a major sports event like the Olympics, the FIFA World Cup, or the European Nations Championship raised levels of life satisfaction in the nations concerned and, second, to test whether performing above expectations at these events (based on medal predictor indices and international football rankings) might also raise happiness. They used the Eurobarometer survey, which has been taken twice a year for several decades and which covers 12 European countries. The results showed that team performances had little impact on levels of life satisfaction, but hosting was a different matter. Although there was no positive effect on Spanish or Greek happiness from hosting the Barcelona and Athens Olympics in 1992 and 2004, however, hosting a major soccer tournament had positive effects, estimated at 50% greater than those emanating from being married. Nevertheless, marriage can last a long time, unlike the feel-good factor from hosting a mega-event, which was essentially short-term in its impact. Whether we can generalise from the European experience, a continent that is immersed in soccer, to the rest of the globe is conjectural, but soccer is reputedly the world game.

Dolan et al. (2019) have assessed intangible benefits applicable to the London Games of 2012 by asking Londoners about their level of life satisfaction, happiness, and anxiety. They used an 11-point Likert scale, viewed as more reliable than shorter scales, in which zero equated to 'not at all' and ten inferred 'completely'. No questions were asked about the Olympics themselves. As a control, interviews were also held with Parisians and Berliners, and in total, over 26,000 people were interviewed. The findings suggested that hosting the Games had a positive effect on the well-being of London residents, to the extent of perhaps £650 worth of life satisfaction per individual, or an aggregate amount of between £2.2 billion and £7 billion, depending on what assumptions were made. Whether this was sufficient to justify the expense of hosting was less clear. When Londoners alone were considered, it was not, but if there was any spillover of positive welfare to the rest of the United Kingdom, a case could be argued. However, there was no long-term legacy of intangible benefits which, at most, lasted for perhaps a year. One interesting finding was that life satisfaction also increased during the London Olympics for residents of Paris and Berlin, which leads to the idea that it might be best to let other cities take on the costs of hosting and *free-ride* on the benefits of their spending. An altruistic alternative would be to cooperate and share the costs between several cities, though I suspect that this would be a political non-starter.

How about just playing sport as a source of happiness for the participants (ignoring sliced drives and missed putts)? Two pioneering studies looked, respectively, at England and the United States in the early twenty-first century. Forrest and McHale (2010) used a survey carried out in England in 2005/2006 covering 27,989 adults who rated their state of happiness from one to ten and, among other things, whether or not they had participated in sport in the four weeks preceding their questioning. These economists took a narrow definition and excluded any physical activity which they felt was more of a recreational pastime – such as fishing, skiing, swimming, and yachting – rather than competitive sport. Sports participants reported higher levels of happiness than non-participants (0.25 happiness points), though, as this could be due to differences in the composition of the two groups, the results were controlled for major variables, such as income, marital status, religion, and unemployment. Nevertheless, the sports group still came out happier (0.11 happiness points). Similar results were found for the United States by Huang and Humphreys (2010) who mined some 1.2 million respondents to the Centers for Disease Control and Prevention's Behavioral Risk Factor Surveillance Survey (now there's a mouthful!).

Yet the question remains as to whether those who choose to play sport are happier individuals in themselves and would be still happier than most even if they did not get to participate in sport. One way that this has been assessed is by calculating the happiness levels of those living in reasonable proximity to sports facilities (defined in one study as within 20 minutes travel). The conclusion was that access to facilities was a major factor, especially with women, in leading to a greater likelihood of participating in sport, which, in turn, by making them healthier, more active, and more social, was what made them feel even happier. One of the most recent attempts at dealing with this concern that causality cannot be inferred from a correlation has come from Frey and Gullo (2021) who used 13 data sets at different points in time from the longitudinal (and highly detailed) German Socio-Economic Panel. By means of tests (too sophisticated to explain here), they calculated that the impact on happiness of engaging in sport was about four times higher than the reverse causality.

It can therefore be argued that public funding of sports facilities can be justified because of the health and happiness that they bring. Doubtless, politicians would prefer their constituents to be healthy rather than ill and happy rather than sad, but, of course, they have to consider the *opportunity cost* of such spending: could it be more fruitfully expended in other areas? However, while health benefits can be given an economic value, this is less true of happiness, so the question of where to put funds remains a political rather than an economic decision. Moreover, even in grassroots sports funding, governments may have motives other than health and happiness, as was recently demonstrated in Australia when the federal government ignored protocols to give money to sports organisations in marginal seats prior to a general election.

In the past, public spending on sport was often justified by a military doctrine. War was an ever-present likelihood and a nation needed a fit population to fight its wars. Sport could contribute to this, and also some sporting skills, such as archery and rifle-shooting, were readily transferable to the killing fields. The nature of warfare has changed, and nowadays the argument for spending on sport is based more on economics: on the reduction to a nation's physical and mental health bill.

Yet sport is not always good for you: indeed, at times, it can be painful and unpleasant. By extrapolating from available data, Fair and Champa (2019) estimate that male contact sports in US high schools and colleges lead to 617,000 more injuries and 98,000 more healthy years lost than non-contact sports. They calculate that (in 2015 prices) the excess total injury bill was between $433 million and $1.5 billion for colleges and between $5.1 billion and £18.4 billion for high schools. The ranges were due to using costs from two different sources, either those of the National Safety Council or those from the Department of Health and Human Services. More recently, there has been increased concern with concussion in contact sport and the mental health problems of elite sportspersons.

There is also economic sense in playing sport. Sport can increase personal productivity directly by enabling individuals to work longer and harder and indirectly via the experience of being on teams. Rooth's (2011) study of recruits into the Swedish army showed that physical fitness could bring a premium in the labour market of about 4% in earnings later in life, equivalent to the same influence as 1.3 years of work experience or an additional year of schooling. He looked at 446,930 males aged between 28 and 38 in 2003 who had undertaken national service (which was compulsory in Sweden) when they were 18. Using army details of fitness and tax record, he initially came up with a 7% premium which was lowered when he looked only at 144,617 brothers (to allow for any family influences) and also discounted for height within the cohort. In a separate exercise, reported in the same paper, it was found that participation in sport increased the chances of being called for an interview for a position by two percentage points, equivalent to 1.5 years of relevant work experience.

Faith, Hope, and Corporate Social Responsibility

Currently in Britain, there are over 150,000 registered charities associated with sport, mainly small sports clubs but also including the Football Foundation, one of the 50 largest charities in Britain. In the United States, the NFL, one of the world's major sports organisations, committed itself to philanthropic activity over 75 years ago and in 1973 established NFL Charities, the first league-wide foundation in professional sports. Some of the money earned from American college football, in particular the post-season bowl games, has gone to charity. The Peach Bowl has given over $32 million since 2000, the Fiesta Bowl over $12.5 million, and the Rose, Citrus, and Alamo Bowls have spent millions in their communities on college scholarships for lower-income students, affordable housing, and improving city parks in poor neighbourhoods. On a global basis, the Homeless World Cup Foundation was established in 2001 with the aim of using soccer to alleviate homelessness, but it has widened its ambitions to include the promotion of social opportunities and access to support for those experiencing homelessness. Although Scottish-based, it now works in 450 locations and co-ordinates a network of partners in 74 countries and in 2016 was estimated to have created $364 million in social capital. Additionally, charities worldwide have often developed a symbiotic relationship with partners to assist in charitable fundraising. The popularity of sport makes it ideal for such partnerships and, hence, worldwide, we find the creation of specific events for 'piggybacking' on existing sports events for the purpose of making collections, the use of sports stars to raise the profile of particular charities, and the sponsorship of participants, from celebrities to primary school children's involvement in swims with support from grannies and neighbours.

What is surprising is how little economists have looked at sport and charity, especially as the charity sector is in a unique economic position. It differs from the private sector in that revenue is not an end in itself but a resource to be utilised, and it is different from the public sector, as it cannot forcibly raise revenue by taxation (Ott 2001). It is differentiated from both in that its sources of support include volunteer time and donations of money. Until the late twentieth century, economists tended to ignore the non-profit area, dismissing it as an unproductive use of resources and outside the realm of rational economics because it was not profit-focused (Rose-Ackerman 1996). Generally, they now argue that charities exist because of *market failures* in the private sector and voids left by government agencies in the public sector.

Then we have what I call 'charity plus', the policies emanating out of the development of corporate social responsibility (CSR). In 1935, US tax authorities decided that corporations could deduct up to 5% of their pre-tax income for charitable purposes. Although political right wingers still considered such deductions as theft from shareholders, the way was open for a rethink of the role of companies in civil society. Still, for many years, social obligations remained an afterthought, if companies considered them at all, and sports organisations were no different. Slowly, however, came a realisation that CSR was not a zero-sum game. Rather than charitable works costing them money, there could be positive economic spin-offs for clubs and companies as their enhanced reputations encouraged an expansion of their customer base.

The core principle of CSR is that companies have responsibilities to society beyond traditional profit-maximisation. These include acting in a way which contributes positively not just to shareholders but also to all stakeholders, including workers, customers, and the communities within which the enterprises exist. It is this latter aspect that has been seized upon by sports clubs and associations that have realised that teams and organisations, like individual sportspersons, can increase their social standing in the community through philanthropic activities, which in most cases have gone beyond the simple handout to the needy to the organisation of community-based projects with the potential for positive social impact. In the past two decades, especially in North America, where elite sports teams are run more for profit than in Europe, professional sports executives have become increasingly concerned with the image, reputation, and public perception of their teams and have attempted to integrate them into the communities which they purport to represent (Walker et al. 2016). In essence, these clubs and organisations have engaged in strategic philanthropy, and CSR has become an important part of their business activities: doing good has been good for business. What has emerged is that a club can use its resources to achieve both profits and social benefits: the two are not incompatible. Most major league teams in the United States have charitable work written into their mission statements, and their players are contractually obliged to become involved (though compulsory voluntary work sounds oxymoronic). Moreover, the leading sports agencies will not take on athletes unless they agree to establish a charitable foundation or volunteer their time and/or money towards charitable purposes: for them, favourable publicity brings in the endorsement dollars. This is not to say that the players do not want to help and do something that can improve lives, just to note that there are economic benefits to having a good reputation.

Yet we have no real idea how effective CSR has been, as there has been a broad failure to evaluate the impact of programmes other than to count the number of individuals dealt with. Manchester City F.C., an organisation that has been involved in community programmes for over three decades, does make estimates of the return per pound invested in schemes that have reduced anti-social behaviour and improved the health of disabled young people, but they are a rarity. Too many clubs and associations simply show how much they have spent on what they believe is self-evidently 'a good thing'.

The COVID-19 pandemic has brought into focus the local community charity work undertaken by many sports bodies. EPL clubs, for example, expended an average of about £3 million per club, the equivalence of the annual salary of one of their players (Kennedy and Kennedy 2021). Whether you think this is a large or small amount may depend on your political outlook.

Sport for Development

Over the past couple of decades, the sports world has seen the emergence of a nascent socio-political movement (with economic implications) into a recognised field focusing on Sport for Development and Peace, usually abbreviated to SDP. This involves the deliberate use of sport and physical activity to attain specific development objectives, usually in lower-income nations but sometimes in pockets of deprivation in higher-income ones. The objectives generally concentrate on the areas of child and youth development, aspects of health, gender equality, social inclusion, educational development, and post-conflict resolution. There can be a diverse set of entities involved, generally with no overarching control, ranging from United Nations agencies to faith schools. Generally, economists have not had much to say about SDP. A recent survey of the literature on SDP economics scarcely garnered a mention (Peachey et al. 2020), though recently Whitley (2019) has advocated the application of behavioural economics by funders to bring about change in SDP organisations, particularly in encouraging them to prioritise longer-term considerations.

The main international stakeholders have been intergovernmental organisations, especially agencies of the United Nations whose involvement in SDP began in 2001 with the appointment of a special advisor in the area. Later, the United Nations established an Inter-Agency Task Force in 2002 and a Working Group in 2004, resulting, in 2005, in a designated United Nations Office for Sport and Development (UNOSDP). There followed an outpouring of policy documents and resolutions, unfortunately not matched by action in the field. In a surprising move in 2017, UNOSDP was closed and a new relationship established with IOC. However, the IOC has done relatively little, unlike, for all its faults, FIFA, which has financed a significant number of football-related SDP projects throughout the developing world. All these agencies suffer from the issue of whether the richer nations are using the clout of their funding to promote their own ideologies: is it just a newer version of colonialism?

Some of the SDP projects impinge on education, health, and other fields which ultimately are the province of government. Here there is the problem of a hangover of colonialism in which one side thinks it knows best and the other rejects any imposition of ideas from external sources. Then there is the basic issue of the prioritisation of winning medals within the sports policies of emerging nations (one idea they have adopted from wealthier countries). Much more influential (in a positive way) within most countries have been non-government organisations, but they suffer from short-termism in continually having to seek funds to keep their projects afloat.

Advocates of SDP would not see it as charitable work but as assisting individuals and communities with helping themselves to improve their own life chances. They postulate sport as a *merit good*, one that ought to be consumed but which suffers a shortfall in demand (remembering that demand is always a demand for a good at a particular price) because potential consumers do not have enough income or, to use the taste variable, do not appreciate the benefits of participation and thus do not rate it highly in their spending priorities.

One overarching issue is that the idea that sports participation can have beneficial effects on child development (via youth empowerment, health promotion, educational attainment, and general well-being) has been based on studies from the developed world. So although sport has been seized upon as a low-cost, potentially high-impact tool for child and youth development elsewhere, there has been a failure to take due regard of the prevailing socio-economic infrastructure. Perhaps the beneficial effects in the United States, Europe, and Australia were not simply because of sport but partially attributable to the quality of educational institutions, social networks, levels of nutrition, and civil organisations. That said, some benefits may still accrue from sports participation in developing areas, as shown in the longitudinal study of children in Peru. By comparing 638 individuals of the same cohort in 2002, 2006, and 2009, Pawlowski et al. (2018) were able to demonstrate that playing sport may have positive effects on social capital (neighbourhood trust, friends' support, and a safe environment) and on health (body mass index and general health status). However, there were no statistically significant effects on well-being (satisfaction with life) or human capital formation (school enrolment and improved vocabulary). Readers should note that the methodology was not just a matter of comparing the results of the group that played sport with those of non-sporting children. Allowance had to be made for other factors that might have differentially influenced the results if they were more prominent in one group rather than the other. These included the gender of the child, whether they lived in a rural or urban location, and the level of poverty they experienced.

Clearly, children need protection. They need it within sport to safeguard themselves from predatory coaches; they need it around sport to prevent exploitation in the supply of sports equipment; they need it through sport, such as being taught how to swim to save some of the 17,000 Bangladeshi children aged one to five who drown each year. Some steps have been taken. To help protect children from trafficking, FIFA now bans the transfer of under-18 footballers to other countries unless the parents have relocated for non-footballing reasons or the players already live within 100 kilometres of the new club, and the new club must meet criteria relating to education, living conditions, and general support. Every country in the world but one has signed the United Nations Convention on Children's Rights: the exception is the United States, which claims that to do so would contravene its constitution. This is the country where kids are made to play like adults in a $15 billion a year youth sports economy. In the past, children played games; now they are forced to play sport, often with that obvious form of overt child abuse: the ugly parent screaming on the sidelines. When will UNESCO take this challenge on?

As with CSR, one constant problem with SDP is a failure to adequately assess its impact, with greater emphasis given to measuring inputs than outcomes. Too often, social enterprise organisations simply believe that they are doing good and lack critical assessment or even reflection. Overall, SDP has been piecemeal in its impact: a good idea thwarted by politics and practicalities. In 2013/2014, the revenues of the big-five European soccer leagues aggregated over $11 billion (Plumley et al. 2017). Five years later, this was still larger than the GDPs of 62 countries of the 192 listed by the World Bank World Development Indicators. Sport cannot put this right. It can contribute but its effects will be miniscule compared to the impact of more beneficial trade and less exploitative inward investment

References

Depetris-Chauvin, Emilio, Ruben Durante and Filipe Campante (2020), 'Building Nations through Shared Experiences: Evidence from African Football', *American Economic Review* 110.5, 1572–1602.

Dolan, Paul, et al (2019), 'Quantifying the Intangible Impact of the Olympics Using Subjective Well-Being Data', *Journal of Public Economics* 177, 104043.

Fair, Roy C. and Christopher Champa (2019), 'Estimated Costs of Contact in College and Hoigh School Male Sports', *Journal of Sports Economics* 20.5, 690–717.

Forrest, David and Ian G. McHale (2010), 'Subjective Well-Being and Engagement in Sport: Evidence From England' in Plácido Rodríguez, Stefan Késenne and Brad R. Humphreys (eds.), *The Economics of Sport, Health and Happiness* (Edward Elgar: Cheltenham), 184–199.

Frey, Bruno S. and Anthony Gullo (2021), 'Does Sport Make People Happier, or Do Happy People More Sports? [sic]', Journal of Sports Economics 22.4, 432–458.

Huang, Haifang and Brad R. Humphreys (2010), 'Sports Participation and Happiness: Evidence From Us Micro Data' in Plácido Rodríguez, Stefan Késenne and Brad R. Humphreys eds., *The Economics of Sport, Health and Happiness* (Edward Elgar: Cheltenham), 163–183.

Kavetsos, Georgios and Stefan Szymanski, 'National Well-Being and International Sports Events', *Journal of Economic Psychology* 31 (2010), 158–171.

Kennedy, David and Peter Kennedy (2021), 'English Premier League Football Clubs During the Covid-19 Pandemic: Business as Usual?', *Soccer and Society* 22.1–2, 1–8.

Morton, R. Hugh (2000), 'Who Won the Sydney 2000 Olympics?: An Allometric Approach', *The Statistician* 51.2, 147–155

Ott, J. Steven (2001), *The Nature of the Nonprofit Sector* (Westview: Colorado).

Pawlowski, Tim, Ute Schüttoff, Paul Downward and Michael Lechner (2018), 'Can Sport Really Help to Meet the Millennium Development Goals? Evidence From Children in Peru', *Journal of Sports Economics* 19.4, 498–521.

Peachey, Jon Welty, Nico Schulenkorf and Patrick Hill (2020), 'Sport-for Development: A Comprehensive Analysis ofTheoretical and Conceptual Advancements', *Sport Management Review* 23.5, 783–796.

Plumley, Daniel, Robert Wilson and Simon Shibli (2017), 'A Holistic Performance Assessment of English Premier League Football Clubs 1992–2013', *Journal of Applied Sports Management* 9.1, 1–24.

Rewilak, Johan (2021), 'The (Non) Determinants of Olympic Success', *Journal of Sports Economics* 22.5, 546–570.

Rooth, Dan-Olof (2011), 'Work Out or Out ofWork: The Labour Market Return to Physical Fitness and Leisure Sports Activities', *Labour Economics* 18, 399–409.

Rose-Ackerman, Susan (1996), 'Altruism, Nonprofits, and Economic Theory', *Journal of Economic Literature* 34.2, 701–728.

Walker, Matthew, Bob Heere and Kim Chiyoung (2016), 'The Paradox of CSR Measurement: Putting the Responsibility Back Into CSR Through Program Evaluation' in Juan Luis Paramio-Salcines, Kathy Babiak and Geoff Walters (eds.), *Routledge Handbook of Sport and Corporate Social Responsibility* (Routledge: Abingdon), 309–316.

Whitley, Meredith A. (2019), 'Behavioral Economics in Sport For Development and Peace: A Viable Route to Innovation?', *Managing Sport and Leisure* 24.1–3, 173–192.

14

CORRUPTION, ENVIRONMENTAL UNSUSTAINABILITY, AND DISCRIMINATION

Cheating in Sport

From an economist's point of view, sport is a contest in which competitors respond to incentives. However, sometimes these incentives are so desired that participants are tempted 'to cheat to win' in order to secure the rewards, be they financial or psychic. Such cheating normally takes the form of sabotaging one's opponents or taking performance-enhancing substances. Economists argue that economic actors seek to maximise what is termed *utility*, which can be gauged in financial terms, using both real and *psychic income*. The latter infers a value that individuals place on personal kudos, honour, or other nonpecuniary rewards. Economists have developed formulaic models to explain corruption in sport as a rational decision-making process in which a potentially corrupt individual weighs various probabilities (e.g. Maennig 2006; Forrest et al. 2008). You may recoil in horror from a formula mentioned in the chapter on economists and their tools. This formula was a shortcut (for those who understand such things) to explain how and why sportspersons make a decision whether or not to cheat, take drugs, or throw a game. If you can force yourself to flip back to the offending page, it showed that essentially what they do is undertake a personal *cost-benefit analysis* (as in the mega-events chapter) to determine their best course of action. The individual has legal and illicit alternatives for action and chooses the course of action which, at the time, promises the greatest personal net utility. Any rewards have to be sufficiently high to render the utility higher than the expected disutility (which includes the chances of being caught and the penalty if found guilty) plus the value of the moral threshold. What also has to be considered is the *time preference* of sportspeople: aware that careers in sport can be short, some might put short-term success ahead of long-term health damage and career-threatening detection. All players can be subject to temptation but not all choose to eat the forbidden fruit, though this is not because they are necessarily

DOI: 10.4324/9781003128632-14

incorruptible. To quote a pioneer in the field of the economics of crime, 'some persons become "criminals" not because their basic motivation differs from that of other persons, but because their (perceived) benefits and costs differ' (Becker 1968).

Running Too Fast: Performance-Enhancing Drugs

Economic studies on tackling doping in sport have focused on whether priority should go to improving the detection rates (the preferred option of sports authorities) or increasing the penalties for malfeasants (the preferred option of clean athletes), both of which would act primarily on the negative side of the personal cost-benefit calculation. Lessening the rewards for professional athletes never seems to have been considered, but it is worth noting that, even though the Olympics offers no prize money, so great are the external rewards for winning a gold medal that doping remains a challenge to the organisers. There are some elaborate theoretical models developed which show that stricter doping regulations might actually increase the level of doping by the less talented athletes. Such sportspersons stand to gain more if the superiorly talented ones pull back from doping when the chances of being caught and punished increase, as the latter have a higher *opportunity cost* (in that they stand to lose more as they could have done well even without doping) (Music 2020). In any case, less able athletes, aware that they can never win clean, will always be tempted to dope to have any chance of winning some prize money. They have no incentive to compete clean. Yet none of the models seem to consider how efficiently an athlete dopes. Even the classic situation, in which all athletes dope to level the playing field as they believe all others are doping and, hence, theoretically, no one gains an advantage, ignores the physiological point that athletes' bodies will respond differently to drugs and that some of them will improve their performance more than others. What is clear is that anti-doping has become a significant sector in the sports industry, one that consumes economic resources that might be more productively used elsewhere in sport. Overall, we still do not know how effective anti-doping regulations have been in reducing drug taking.

You may recall that, in an earlier chapter, I noted that players could improve their *personal human capital* by learning valuable skills and work habits from their teammates. However, they could also learn to cheat. The premise is that once one worker adopts questionable methods, others may follow, and a contagion effect makes it sub-culturally acceptable. Gould and Kaplan (2011) examine the negative ethical influence of star baseballer (and later self-admitted drug cheat) Jose Canseco on his fellow players on seven teams with which he played. After controlling for a mass of variables, including managerial quality, ballpark characteristics, and experience, they concluded that a significant number of players had improved performances. A test using 30 comparable players from other teams found no evidence of similar improvements being generated. After the MLB introduced random drug testing and the imposition of penalties for steroid use, the peer effect of Canseco disappeared, which is consistent with the knowledge of steroids gained from Canseco becoming obsolete.

Sports authorities often argue that doping undermines the integrity of their sport and will drive away consumers. There is little evidence of this. Cisyk (2020) shows that when a player was suspended for drug offences in the MLB between 2006 and 2012, there was an immediate 9.3% reduction in the television viewing audience for the offender's team, but this had disappeared after roughly 37 days (or 33 games). Significantly, if the same players were out through injury, there was no such adverse viewing reaction.

Running Too Slow: Match-Fixing

Sporting competition is a process that establishes a hierarchy among participants: put simply, it has winners and losers. Yet the essence of sport is that these results cannot be predicted with total accuracy and should certainly not be predetermined. If this becomes obvious, then audiences will diminish and the event becomes unviable. Spectators and viewers are not the only ones interested in an uncertain result. It is not conducive to gambling that the race should always go to the swiftest, the fight to the strongest, or victory to the most talented. Such predictability of outcome does not create a betting market, as every potential bettor knows who will win. If the result is predictable, there is no betting market; equally, if corruption renders form and skill meaningless, bettors will also withdraw. Yet, having undertaken a personal cost-benefit analysis, some participants respond to incentives not to win and 'cheat to lose' via match-fixing.

Two major reasons for this lie in the money that individuals make (or sometimes do not make) from their sporting endeavours. Attention has been given to the differentials between pecuniary rewards for being corrupt and non-corrupt on the premise that when players are paid badly to perform well, the alternative of being paid well to play badly could prove attractive. The English footballers who fixed games in the 1950s and 1960s were subject to maximum wage legislation until 1961 and de facto restrictions on journeymen wages in the immediate ensuing years, both of which prevented them earning their full *economic rents*; the low pay of Pakistani players was a contributory factor in the corruption problems of that country's cricket; the poor rewards for many British racehorse trainers tempted them to make use of inside information (Vamplew 2018). A second aspect of income affecting corruption decisions, particularly in individual sports, is the distribution of prize money. Where it is allocated significantly asymmetrically, it may incentivise players to try harder and win more, but paradoxically, it may also make a guaranteed sum as a bribe for underperforming an attractive alternative incentive (Muehlhuesser 2006). A prime example here was sumo wrestling in the late twentieth century. Rankings after each of the six annual tournaments in which 15 wrestlers fought each other determined a wrestler's social status and monthly income. Each victory was worth about 3 points, except the eighth win, which offered over 11 points. This nonlinearity of rewards meant that in the crucial bout when a wrestler had seven wins, he stood to gain much more than his opponent stood to lose, a situation which provided an opportunity for possible match-fixing. Duggan and Levitt (2002) examined some 32,000 bouts and showed that approximately 26.0% of all wrestlers finished with exactly eight victories and only 12.2% with seven, whereas the statistical expectation would have been for a frequency of 19.6% in both cases. Moreover, on the last day of the tournament, wrestlers with seven wins were victorious roughly 25% more often than would have been predicted. A suspicion of similar *barter corruption* has been raised by Jetter and Walker (2017) regarding tennis players on the cusp of qualifying for a Grand Slam entry which was dependent on the gaining of ranking points in the preceding tournament.

Competition corruption in the form of match-fixing takes two major forms: one intrinsic to the competition being played and the other involving external influences, such as bookmakers or gamblers. The former is usually for sporting reasons (semantically 'unsporting' might be more technically correct) where a team or individual bribes the opposition to lose so that they can win a competition, gain promotion, or avoid relegation. Alternatively, teams or individuals might opt to underperform to improve their draft selection position or obtain a better handicap for future events. Money lay behind the other major category of match-fixing: that associated with betting fraud. Here gamblers or bookmakers find ways (positive incentives, such as bribes, or negative ones like threats) to persuade an individual or a team to underperform in a particular event so that their knowledge of this gives them an edge in the betting markets.

Corruption is hidden action which distorts the allocation of resources away from competitive outcomes. Successful match-fixing or drug taking is covert: no one boasts about it at the time. Sport authorities have sought to combat the taking of performance-enhancing drugs by increasing the volume of dope testing and hence the likelihood of a doper being caught. Match-fixing has no such testing mechanism, but in recent years, economists using large databases have identified possible patterns of match-fixing by using probability theory. Rodenberg and Feuste (2014) examined nearly 50,000 ATP and WTA tennis matches and concluded that there was a tanking rate of around 1%, a similar level of corruption found by Wolfers (2006) in his study of possible points shaving in NCAA basketball in which he used 44,120 observations. Basketball also featured in Taylor and Trogdon's (2002) examination of nearly 6,000 matches in the NBA, which concluded that the reverse order draft system encouraged teams to lose games to improve their draft position once all chance of reaching the play-offs had gone. For fuller details of these and other instances, see Vamplew (2018).

Several observers believe that fixing is on the increase, if not in actual match-fixing (though this is likely), most certainly in spot-fixing (first free kick, first yellow card, etc.) which, like point shaving allows a corrupt athlete to underperform but not necessarily lose. Andreff (2018) maintains that a dark market has emerged in which corrupt sportspersons on the supply side are taking the initiative in selling out the sport. The underlying logic behind this belief is the vast growth in global betting taking advantage of the internet and the deregulation of many gambling markets.

Running Too Much: Destroying the Environment

Environmental issues emerged as a major international concern in the last quarter of the twentieth century with sustainability becoming a catchcry for protecting the future. Sport, however, came late to the sustainability party: indeed, for decades, golf clubs in particular were in denial about golf's adverse environmental effects. Now, however, economic self-interest has forced many clubs, leagues, and organisations to adopt eco-friendly policies for their activities (Sanderson and Shaikh 2017). Generally, sound environmental stewardship can reduce environmental degradation, maintain liveable environments, and ensure the long-term health of the sports industry as a whole. More specifically, taking informed steps towards environmental responsibility can result in substantial economic benefits to sport via more efficient use of resources and an enhanced public image. Sanderson and Shaikh (2017) suggest that five things matter when sporting organisations are considering environmental investments.

- Whether it will yield any *direct private return*, such as the additional profit that can accrue from the lower operating costs associated with increased energy efficiencies
- *Indirect private return* emanating from an improved public image via more customers, better labour relations, and sponsorship deals
- *Social benefits* going to those who do not bear the cost of the investment and how this is perceived by those who are paying
- Some investments might stem from *government interventions* to force or encourage the investment to be undertaken via penalties or subsidies
- Finally, there is the question of *subsidies* to sports organisations, in particular the provision of municipally owned stadiums, which might require investment in (say) green space as part of the deal

Mega-event organisers, perhaps to assuage their guilt, now demand environmental statements from potential hosts. From 1991, the IOC Charter was amended to ensure that future Games must take account of the fragile nature of the environment, and in 1994, the United Nations Environment Programme created a sports and environment unit to evaluate the impact of hosting Olympic events. This may or may not have influenced decisions to award the Games to particular hosts. It may all be window dressing. There is no recorded instance of the IOC or FIFA or any other promoter of sporting mega-events taking retrospective action to punish hosts who failed to meet their environmental targets. That said, the Vancouver Winter Games of 2010 emphasised environmental stability. Many venues collected rainwater for irrigation use and captured heat from used bath and shower water; almost 70% of the heating for the Olympic Village was provided by waste heat recovery systems; mass transit and cycling were encouraged as alternatives to using cars.

Nevertheless, it remains true that sport is bad for the environment. Nothing that sport does has positive consequences for the climate or the environment. At best, sport participation and spectatorship can be neutral; at worst, they can be devastating. The sport on which environmental activists have focused is golf, a land-hungry sport with a standard 18-hole course requiring some 80–100 acres of land. In itself, this might not be too bad environmentally if wildlife, both flora and fauna, were encouraged to inhabit the area. In practice, however, golf's environmental impact is negative, involving water use, land depletion, and toxic contamination, though golfers do appear to be willing to pay a premium to play on an environmentally friendly course. Limehouse et al. (2010) compared the green fees of the 1,179 courses in the United States (some 6.9% of total courses) that had environmental accreditation from the independent Audubon organisation with a sample from other courses. Given that every course has its own peculiarities, the researchers estimated *hedonic prices* (remember them from Chapters 7 and 10) for various aspects of a round of golf, including yardage, rating, slope, on-site professional, and the availability of caddies to determine the extra charges paid to play on an environmentally certified course. They concluded that golfers seem willing to pay a premium of 10%–18% a round. Additional to the environmental issues where golf already exists is that of course construction in the developing world, both as a response to golf tourism and to increasing domestic demand from wealthier inhabitants for high-status leisure pursuits. This often involves the destruction of natural landscape, deforestation, and clearing of vegetation, leading to gullying and erosion. Nevertheless, neither golf nor sport in aggregate will be the tipping point into environmental disaster: the world's eco-system has much more to fear from industrial producers and insatiable consumers.

The degraded environment may have its revenge on sport as climate change lessens the opportunity for winter sports, causes flooding of sports grounds across the world, and harms players forced to compete in high temperatures or poor air quality. This is not all in the distant future. Already an average marathon runner would have needed an extra 12 minutes to complete the Beijing Marathon of 2014 than on a day with normal air quality (which from my personal experience – being in Beijing not marathon running – is still not that good). A study of over 300,000 runners in 56 Chinese marathon races in 2014 and 2015 pointed out the obvious fact that times lengthened as air quality deteriorated (Guo and Shihe 2019), but by quantifying their results, the authors were able to contribute statistically to establishing the detrimental effect of air pollution on short-term productivity, which could have relevance not just to sport but also the wider economy.

Not Running at All: Discrimination

Any moral stance against discrimination taken by economists should be as members of society not because of being economists. Economics should be morally neutral, but it can be used to explain the consequences of behaviours and decisions that many might find abhorrent. Discrimination is a case in point. When economists talk of discrimination in professional sport, they are concerned with inequality of access to a sport and unequal salaries for equal work. To them, discrimination is an action whereby people from different demographic groups with equal abilities and productivity are rewarded differently. This results from prejudice, which is a taste for a particular form of *utility* that brings satisfaction to the individual concerned. Here we will mainly focus on racial discrimination, but the points raised are applicable to other forms of exclusion, segregation, and prejudicial treatment.

Discrimination on the grounds of race is not sporting corruption (though it may be illegal), but it certainly demonstrates sporting dysfunction. The denial of access to sport can be absolute, as in the MLB in the United States, where no black player featured from the 1880s to 1947. Ironically, this benefitted the Negro Leagues (no PC in those days), which were able to hire star-quality black players and attract crowds wanting to see the best in action. When the colour line was broken in the MLB, these leagues lost their best black players and folded. While the colour line in professional football was more fluid, no blacks played in the NFL from 1934 to 1945. Even in integrated teams, discrimination in access to work can occur on racial grounds. Selection processes such as the North American draft, in which clubs reveal their preferences for players in order of priority, demonstrate this, partly because some owners and managers can hold stereotyped views of players' suitability for certain positions. Blacks were often relegated to speed and strength positions and not chosen for positions of influence and decision-making, such as quarterback in American football and pitcher or catcher in baseball (Conlin and Patrick 2006).

Discrimination in elite sport is generally considered to be economically irrational, as it deprives a team of potentially better players. When the colour barrier in baseball was broken, it was those clubs which integrated first that secured the better results. Similarly in English soccer, between 1978 and 1993, teams with more black players won more frequently (Szymanski 2000). In effect, the owners of less-integrated teams were prepared to sacrifice the kudos of a successful season for the utility of enforcing their racial prejudices. That said, it is possible that discrimination was a rational business decision, as it was argued that spectator prejudice against black players, especially in the segregated southern states of America, would have undermined baseball's consumer base.

Under-representation of a demographic group is often seen as an indicator that racial or ethnic discrimination is operating, but there could be other explanations. For example, an analysis by Cranfield et al. (2016) of the relative lack of French Canadians in the NHL used a database of 5,130 players drafted from 1970 to 2008 who played at least one game. Instead of attributing this to an ethnic preference for marketing reasons – as was the conventional explanation – they brought in a new element, the physical size of players and demonstrated that over the entire twentieth century, French-Canadian players were significantly smaller in both height and weight than those from the rest of Canada.

And what of the reverse position where minorities are over-represented, as in the early 1990s when black soccer players made about 8% of appearances in the elite English football leagues but were only 2% of the English population at the time. Does this demonstrate enlightened soccer ownership in England? Only if it could be shown that they were being paid the same as white players of equal ability and that has not been established (Szymanski 2000). Even prejudiced owners will employ players from non-favoured groups if they are willing to work for a lower salary than those in the preferred group. Remember profits are income less costs, so if costs can be reduced without adversely affecting performance, then profits might be increased. In basketball in the 1980s, despite 75% of players being black, whites had a 20% salary advantage (Groothuis and Richard Hill 2004). More recently, in a variation of the usual racial prejudice seen in American sport, European basketball players in the NBA might earn up to 17.4% less than identically productive US-born players (Yang and Lin 2012).

What this means is that discriminatory owners and managers are prepared to put a price on their discrimination, the difference in what they are prepared to pay (say) a black player compared to a white player. Their prejudice means that they feel one is worth more than the other. In practice, they are getting the discriminated-against player cheaper than their productivity would warrant. One way to look at it is that black and white players are in segmented labour markets where whites and blacks are not competing for places against each other but solely against members of their own racial group. Within each group, there is a maximum salary that will be paid, but it is higher in the white group. However, in an integrated team, the owner might be prepared to bid for the discriminated-against player and pay a higher wage to improve his own team's performance. To retain such players (they may be of a different race but their contribution is considered important), the discriminator would then have to improve their own wage offers. However, to maintain the pay gap which their prejudice requires, they would have to overpay their preferred racial group. Once you pay more than their productivity warrants, you are on economically shaky ground.

All professionals face the situation where the physical effects of age begin to outweigh the experience gained, but does race influence the decision for some careers to be terminated earlier than others? Such exit discrimination could have a greater financial impact on players than wage discrimination (Hoang and Rascher 1999). Groothuis and Richard Hill's (2004) study of 1,113 players found that in the decade from 1989, the average NBA career was 6 years for white players and 5.5 for black. Yet the deciding factor was not race: measured by game metrics (points, blocks, rebounds, etc.), more productive players were retained irrespective of race, with size being the key variable, and white players tended to be bigger by 2 inches and 14 pounds than their black counterparts. This supports the evidence emerging from the literature, which suggests that from the early 1990s, economic discrimination was on the decline in North American major league sports. Winning games superseded the racial prejudices of fans.

Economists have tended to ignore discrimination at the grassroots level, but clearly, sports clubs have preferred to be homogeneous rather than heterogeneous. Members generally want to play and socialise (a significant feature of club life) with like-minded individuals. This is freedom of choice in operation. However, it becomes less economically rational if there is an economic cost attached to such behaviour. Once this becomes apparent, attitudes might not change, but behaviours often do. More generally in Britain, since overt discrimination on the grounds of gender was made a condition of ineligibility for lottery grants or Sports Council funding, many male and female sports associations merged to ensure they were not excluded from applying for such aid. In the United States, the country club, long the luxurious refuge of whites at play, finally began to end discrimination against minorities, as previously inappropriate members became economically more important. Increased taxation on club fees, their removal as a tax-deductible business expense, and the increased geographical mobility of many Americans (which cut the desire to establish local roots) forced a rethink, as white membership alone could no longer keep them afloat.

Some are excluded from watching or participating simply because they cannot afford to buy a ticket or purchase equipment. This rationing by price is not usually seen as discrimination but simply the free market at work, with suppliers of matches, venues, and goods needing to cover their costs and make a profit. Somehow (and this is my moral judgement), the poor are blamed for being poor, unlike those excluded because of their gender, race, or ethnicity where the finger is more likely to be pointed at the discriminator.

Sport and Crime: A Parting Shot

The sports world, with its reward structures, association with gambling, international money flows, and opaque operating systems, is one in which criminality and corruption can flourish (Andreff 2018). Indeed, though without making specific allegations (for legal reasons?), Carin and Terrien (2020) argue that a rational explanation of the ownership changes in French football clubs (as occurred in 22 of the 40 top division clubs between 2010/2011 and 2018/2019) despite recurring deficits (aggregating €657 million in the same period) is the ability to launder dirty money through their financial operations. In other words, the corporate strategy is neither *profit-maximisation* nor *utility maximisation* (as defined earlier) but a means to aid criminal activity. Implicit in their argument is that this could apply to any elite sports club in which the rate of return is insufficient to attract conventional investors.

References

Andreff, Wladimir (2018), 'Different Types of Manipulation in Sport' in Markus Breuer and David Forrest (eds.), *The Palgrave Handbook of the Economics of Manipulation in Professional Sports* (Palgrave Macmillan: London), 13–35.

Becker, Gary (1968), 'Crime and Punishment: An Economic Approach', *Journal of Political Economy* 76.2, 169–217.

Carin, Yann and Mickael Terrien (2020), 'A Game Without Penalty: Purchasing a Professional Club, a Rational Crime?', *Quality in Sport* 4.6, 38–53.

Cisyk, Jeffrey (2020), 'Impacts of Performance-Enhancing Drug Suspensions on the Demand for Major League Baseball', *Journal of Sports Economics* 21.4, 391–419.

Conlin, Michael and M. Emerson Patrick (2006), 'Discrimination in Hiring versus Retention and Promotion: An Empirical Analysis of Within-Firm Treatment of Players in the NFL', *Journal of Law, Economics & Organization* 22.1, 115–136.

Cranfield, John, Kris Inwood and J. Andrew Ross (2016), 'Ethnic Inequality in Professional Sport: A Question of Discrimination in the National Hockey League Draft' in Richard Pomfret and John K. Wilson (eds.), *Sports Through the Lens of Economic History* (Edward Elgar: Cheltenham), 128–141.

Duggan, Mark and Stephen D. Levitt (2002), 'Winning Isn't Everything: Corruption in Sumo Wrestling', *American Economic Review* 92.5, 383–396.

Forrest, David, Ian McHale and Kevin McAuley (2008), '"Say It Ain't So": Betting-Related Malpractice in Sport', *International Journal of Sport Finance* 3, 156–166.

Gould, Eric D. and Todd R. Kaplan (2011), 'Learning Unethical Practices from a Co-Worker: The Peer Effect of Jose Canseco', *Labour Economics* 18, 338–48.

Groothuis, Peter A. and J. Richard Hill (2004), 'Exit Discrimination in the NBA: A Duration Analysis of Career Length', *Economic Inquiry* 42.2, 341–349.

Guo, Mengmeng and Fu Shihe (2019), 'Running With a Mask? The Effect of Air Pollution on Marathon Runners' Performance', *Journal of Sports Economics* 20.7, 903–928.

Hoang, Ha and Daniel Rascher (1999), 'The NBA, Exit Discrimination and Career Earnings', *Industrial Relations 38*.1, 69–91.

Jetter, Michael and Jay K. Walker (2017), 'Good Girl, Bad Boy? Evidence Consistent with Collusion in Professional Tennis', *Southern Economic Journal* 84.1, 155–180.

Limehouse, Frank E., Peter C. Melvin and Robert E. McCormick (2010), 'The Demand for Environmental Quality: An Application of Hedonic Pricing in Golf', *Journal of Sports Economics* 11.3, 261–286.

Maennig, Wolfgang (2006) 'Corruption' in Wladimir Andreff and Stefan Szymanski (eds.), *Handbook on the Economics of Sport* (Edward Elgar: Cheltenham), 784–794.

Muehlhuesser, Gerd (2006), 'Implications From the Theory of Contests for Modelling and Designing Sports Competitions' in Wladimir Andreff and Stefan Szymanski (eds.), *Handbook on the Economics of Sport* (Edward Elgar: Cheltenham), 342–348.

Music, Kasim (2020), 'The Undesirable Consequences of Doping Regulations: Why Stricter Efforts Might Strengthen Doping Incentives', *Journal of Sports Economics* 21.3, 281–303.

Rodenberg, Ryan M. and Elihu D. Feuste (2014), 'Forensic Sports Analytics: Detecting and Predicting Match-Fixing in Tennis', *Journal of Prediction Markets* 8.1, 77–95.

Sanderson, Allen R. and Sabine L. Shaikh (2017), 'Economics, Sports and the Environment: Incentives and Intersections' in Timothy B. Kellison and Brian McCullough (eds.), *Routledge Handbook of Sport and the Environment* (Routledge: Abingdon), 36–52.

Szymanski, Stefan (2000), 'A Market Test for Discrimination in the English Professional Soccer Leagues', *Journal of Political Economy* 108.3, 590–603.

Taylor, Beck A. and Justin D. Trogdon (2002), 'Losing to Win: Tournament Incentives in the National Basketball Association', *Journal of Labor Economics* 20.1, 23–41.

Vamplew, Wray (2018), 'Tanking, Shirking, and Running Dead: The Role of Economics and Large Data Sets in Identifying Competition Corruption and its Causes', *International Journal of the History of Sport* 35.2–3, 141–156.

Wolfers, Justin (2006), 'Point Shaving: Corruption in NCAA Basketball', *American Economic Review* 96.2, 279–283.

Yang, Chih-Hai and Hsuan-Yu Lin (2012), 'Is There Salary Discrimination by Nationality in the NBA? Foreign Talent or Foreign Market', *Journal of Sports Economics* 13.1, 53–75.

15

THE VIRUS AND AFTER

Coping with Crisis

The Sports World Comes to a Stop

In late March 2020, the Tokyo Olympic Games, scheduled for later that year, were postponed until July 2021. COVID-19 had claimed another sporting victim, this time the world's biggest sporting event. Two months earlier, sports events were being cancelled in Asia, but the Western world was not willing to learn from their experience. In March 2020, two English sports events became super-spreaders for coronavirus. An ignorant British government, still believing that handwashing would combat the virus, with a populist prime minister reluctant to risk his popularity by restricting personal freedom, allowed the four-day Cheltenham National Hunt Festival to proceed and Liverpool to entertain Atlético Madrid in a European Cup Tie at Anfield. At Cheltenham, over 60,000 punters a day, crushed together like sardines, created an ideal environment for the virus to spread, but the Jockey Club was unwilling to cancel the meeting (which brought in a significant proportion of its revenue) and took refuge in the government's hesitancy. Elsewhere in Britain, even before the government belatedly intervened, sanity prevailed, and sports bodies and promoters cancelled fixtures. Sport ground to a halt once authorities realised the dangers of large (and even small) crowds aiding the spread of COVID-19 and the difficulties of socially isolating players in teams and changing rooms. Within weeks, British sport had gone into lockdown, following the example of many European countries, yet America, under a president in denial over COVID-19, remained determined to continue to play games. Ultimately, the MLB had a curtailed season, but in the NFL, not a single game was cancelled thanks to a multi-million-dollar investment in infection control. Across the world, some associations voided their leagues, others used points already gained per game to decide titles, and, controversially, promotions and relegations.

DOI: 10.4324/9781003128632-15

Some *substitutes* were available, including re-running old games (but the excitement had gone except for younger viewers and amnesic older ones who don't remember the result), golf tournaments and NASCAR racing on simulators, and synthetic games such as the computerised Grand National (my wife had the winner in our family sweepstake). However, the clamour grew for real televised sport, not least from those organisations that feared having to pay back broadcasting advances. On a personal note, I felt that I quickly resigned myself to no golf or bowls, perhaps because the season had only just started in the former and not at all in the latter. What I did miss was sport on the television, which, I now realise, I almost used as muzak in the background.

Slowly, but still sometimes too quickly, sport recommenced. Matches behind closed doors, once regarded as a punishment, were now seen as financial lifesavers. Other competitions were organised using bubbles for participants, some successfully with the odd hiccup, others like the Indian Premier League eventually being postponed indefinitely. Ironically, the desire of Indian players not to miss the resurrected competition in September 2021 led to them using fear of catching COVID-19 as an excuse to cancel the final test of a pulsating series with England. Formula 1 rescheduled its races to avoid countries with tough quarantine restrictions. Except in tennis, women's sport went to the back of the queue for restarting, and most professional sport reliant on attendances also had to wait.

At the grassroots level, outdoor sports were allowed to restart but under restrictions. My first round of golf involved making a reservation on Wednesday, attending a socially distanced safety seminar on Thursday, before finally playing with one partner the following Monday. I packed in playing lawn bowls because the health and safety rules became too complex. But that was my choice as I could have played. Those who played contact team sports or indoor sports had no such choice. Until the population is widely vaccinated and cheap COVID-19 testing is readily available, much grassroots sport will remain unplayed.

Whether we will be back to normal, or even a new normal, by the time this book is published lies in the lap of the gods, scientists, and, unfortunately, politicians.

We've Been Here Before

The COVID-19 pandemic was not the first time that sport worldwide has had to face up to a possible existential crisis, most recently was the financial crisis of 2008 following the collapse of Baring Brothers. Humphreys (2010) believes that the impact of the crisis on major league sports in the United States was marginal. He argues that most of the influences on demand, such as price, consumer preference, and quality of the event, were unaffected, and even a downturn in consumer incomes did not impinge significantly on stadium attendance or television audiences. Estimates of franchise values actually showed a slight increase, and the only downturn was in premium seat sales and sponsorship, which were hit as businesses cut back on less essential spending. Two clubs did file for bankruptcy, but these were non-representative, as special circumstances applied to their demise. In looking at

Europe, Andreff (2010) focused on grassroots sport as the main sufferer of the crisis. This stemmed directly from the average European country being about 75% dependent for its grassroots sport on spending by households and local authorities, both of which were hit by the crisis. In contrast, clubs in the European soccer leagues (with the exception of Greece) recovered their pre-crisis growth rates as early as 2011 (Terrien et al. 2021).

Looking solely at one sport in one country, Szymanski (2010) argues that English professional football clubs are remarkably stable. He notes that of the 88 Football League clubs in 1923, all but three of them were still in existence at the time of his paper. He contrasts this with the top 100 British companies in 1912, of which only 51 remained in 1995. However, only five of those that had disappeared had actually gone bankrupt and out of business; most had been taken over by rival companies, an option that was forbidden in English football. A better comparison, but one probably impossible to make, would be with smaller enterprises which might actually show football clubs in an even more favourable light. Football clubs have survived because, rather than go bankrupt, they enter into administration, which allows them to abandon their creditors but continue to trade, though often at the cost of relegation, to a lower division. Creditors lose out, shareholders too, but the club continues. Forty English clubs have taken this avenue to deal with financial distress between 1993 and 2009, five of them twice. No other industry could contemplate such a scale of insolvencies, but football clubs survive because of a peculiar form of brand loyalty, which Szymanski labels 'communal attachment', a relationship with their fans who continue to be consumers with little regard to the quality of the product on offer.

Although we have been here before, this time was different. The pandemic crisis was of a different character and order of magnitude. Governments worldwide intervened in sports markets to prohibit or limit crowds and to ban much professional sport and most grassroots involvement.

Size of the Sports Sector

So far in this book, I have avoided the difficult question of how big the sports industry is, but when we are discussing the COVID-19 pandemic and its effect on sport, it is inevitable that size might matter. However, we just don't know the answer to our question. The global sports market has been valued at between $600 billion and $1.5 trillion, which is an enormous margin for error (Mackreth and Bond 2020).

Estimating the contribution of sport to the economy of even one nation let alone contemplating a global aggregation is beset with difficulties (Andreff 2006). First, there is the problem of sport not being a single definitional entry in any national accounts. A pioneering attempt to look at the British economy in the 1980s found seven sectors in which sport was involved (Henley Centre 1986). Efforts to disentangle sport from other public and private spending and placing a value on volunteer activity involve significate 'guesstimates' and inevitable double counting. Then there is the question of inter-industrial linkages. An input-output model created for the Canadian economy in the late 1980s using 36,000 formulae found 15 other industries that purchased the output of the sports good industry within the domestic economy (Andreff 2006). Disregarding any validity issues (and there are many), such attempts have led to several estimates of the proportion of a nation's GDP attributable to sport. Andreff cites studies for Europe from around 1990 that range between 0.6 for Denmark to 1.8 for the Netherlands and Portugal, whereas twenty-first-century figures suggest 2% of global GDP being generated by sport (Thibault 2014). There still remains the issue of what significance can be applied to these figures. One way is to make comparisons with other industries: for example, Germany's 1.4% in 1990 was higher than that same country's textile sector (Andreff 2006). In 2017, it was estimated that in the United States, professional sport turned over about $69 billion, surpassing the film industry (Sánchez et al. 2019).

Sport certainly has become a major commodity in the contemporary global economy with sporting goods, from shoes and sportswear to high-tech fitness computers and video games to footballs and tennis racquets generating a lucrative global trade. At the end of the twentieth century, the European Commission estimated that trade in sports-related activities was on the order of 3% of world trade (Szymanski 2001). In aggregate, amateur sportspersons spend a fortune to participate in their chosen activities: before COVID-19 intervened, the global equipment and apparel market had been estimated to top $82 billion by the end of 2023 (Research Nester 2020).

Despite frequent comments that sport is now big business, nobody knows how big it actually is. We do know the asset values of the major sports clubs; we are aware of player salaries and sportspersons' wealth league tables but whether sport can be classified as 'big business' is a subjective call. The costs of hosting mega-events like the Olympic Games and the FIFA World Cup, large as they might appear to the lay observer, are dwarfed by the turnover of global financial institutions and the corporate giants of the petroleum industry. At the time of writing, the world's most valuable sports group was Manchester City, whose owner in 2020 sold a 10% share to an American private equity firm, Silver Lake, for $500 million, giving an estimated value of around $5 billion for the whole enterprise. Next in line were Manchester United at $2.8 billion and the Brooklyn Nets basketball venture at $2.35 billion. The assets of leading football clubs may appear large but just look at the those of the major oil, financial, and digital media companies.

The Economic Impact of the Pandemic on Sport

We do not know what long-term effects the pandemic will have on the sporting scene. At the professional level, a recent discussion paper by Schmal (2021) has measured the impact of COVID-19 on infected footballers playing in the German and Italian elite leagues. Using a staggered difference-in-differences design, he identifies negative short- and longer-run performance effects. Relative to their pre-infection outcomes, infected players' performance temporarily drops by more than 6%, but over six months later, it is still around 5% lower.

Financially, there are isolated data, much of it newspaper comments about potential damage rather than specific information, and it is impossible to join the dots and make any aggregated estimates. In an effort to secure government aid, many sports bodies pleaded a worst-case scenario. We won't have any real idea until organisations' annual accounts are published, scrutinised, and compared with previous years' figures. Such a comparison is essential so that COVID-19 is not blamed for normal membership churn, typical levels of club insolvency, or average changes in sponsorship. We may get the earliest information from East Asia where COVID-19 disrupted sport first and where the resumption of sporting life also began earliest (Tan and Lee 2020). Ultimately, we may not know the true cost until the COVID-19 pandemic is changed to an endemic disease which is dealt with by annual vaccinations.

There were some beneficiaries from the pandemic, such as Asian baseball finding a home in the US sport broadcasting market and the accelerated growth of the eSports industry (Rogstad 2020; Tan and Lee 2020). However, it is unlikely that this compensated for such losses as the £300 million reported for the British racing industry and the estimated £40 million by the Swedish sport movement during spring 2020 (Andersson et al. 2020). It is estimated that UEFA's pre-COVID-19 reserves of 500 million euros (£432.64 million) will have shrunk to just over 100 million euros (£86.53 million) by 2023 due to the costs incurred in moving the European Championship back by a year – resulting in rebates to broadcasters and sponsors and refunds to ticket holders, plus the cost of COVID-19 testing and mitigation measures for the rescheduled tournament. In the United States, colleges cut back on their non-revenue-raising sports, which has implications for the US Olympic team, particularly in athletics and swimming where college graduates form the bulk of the competitors. Quansah et al. (2020) made the not unexpected prediction that the COVID-19 pandemic would reduce EPL club revenues, which, in turn, would lead to lower player wages, smaller transfer fees, and a reduction in squad market values. However, in putting a quantitative estimate on the loss, they maintained that the impact would be small from a historical perspective with a worst-case scenario of a decline to 2017/2018 levels.

Whether this would hold for lesser leagues and minority sports is conjectural. In Germany, not having a paying crowd affected minor sports much more than those that were able to draw on broadcasting fees for their matches in empty stadiums. In Germany, for example, in 2018/2019, the share of spectator revenue for the Deutsche Fußball Liga (DFL) was close to 13%, but all other German professional sports leagues, such as hockey (32%), handball (26%), and basketball (20%) were much more dependent on crowd revenue. The comparable percentages from media, mainly television contracts, were 66% football, 14% hockey, 14% basketball, and just 2% in handball, with consequent differentials in their ability to raise sponsorship money (Horky 2021).

Perhaps the real sufferers were grassroots sports participants in terms of lower levels of fitness and happiness and higher levels of mental illness. Yet, so far, no one has attempted to calculate the cost of this to individuals and society, though the Australian Sports Foundation, a charitable organisation benefitting local community sport, estimated that local clubs stand to lose A$1.6 billion as subscriptions, sponsorships, catering receipts, and other sources of revenue disappear. We really need to know how many sports clubs were teetering on the brink of insolvency before the pandemic. Terrien et al. (2021) have examined the state of French amateur football (top tier rather than grassroots) and argue that more clubs were in a better position to withstand the economic effects of COVID-19 than at the time of the financial crisis. More studies are needed before we can make any generalisations given the heterogeneity that typifies most non-professional sports organisations. In particular, we require information on the proportion of income that is generated locally (membership fees and gate-money) and the level of public subsidy they are receiving.

Coping with Crisis

Once decisions have been made to cancel or postpone fixtures and events, then certain issues need to be examined, though, hopefully, in well-operated sports businesses there will have been some form of risk assessment and contingent planning. The major problem facing any organisation in times of crisis is cash flow and the need to pay for current outgoings: the failure to manage this is responsible for most bankruptcies and insolvencies.

Looking first at revenues. Gate-money has gone, though season tickets have already been paid for. One issue to be considered, not just on ethical grounds but because they might affect future purchasing decisions, is whether season ticket holders should get a refund for games that were not played or, more likely given short-term financial shortages, a discount on next season's tickets? Some merchandising might continue but only via online sales if non-essential shops have been closed and earnings from non-sports sources for ground facilities such as conferences, receptions, and weddings will disappear. At the elite level, there is the matter of broadcasting contracts: to what extent have the television companies paid in advance, or are there monies still owing which could be drawn upon? All in all, there will be very little coming in. However, if the sport is a seasonal one, there should be experience in dealing with a time of the year with reduced cash flow. Moreover, if the cessation coincided with the closed season (which will vary with the hemispheres), then the problem might be minimised.

Then there are the outgoings such as rents due on properties that have been hired, the servicing of existing debts, but primarily labour costs which dominate the spending of many sports organisations. If players and other staff are prepared to take wage cuts, then there is some relief. The England rugby team agreed to a 25% wage cut for a year. Similarly, deferral of wages can ease the short-run situation, but this does not assist permanently and can even aggravate the problem at a later stage, as ultimately there is no diminution in the expected expenditure. There is an assumption that when sport returns to normal, above-normal revenues will be generated, but how likely is this?

What other lines of financial assistance might be available? Grants are the easiest solution, but there will be a longer-term cost to either the taxpayers if they are government funded or to the constituent clubs of a sports association if the bailout comes from their governing body. There is no such thing as a free lunch, with the exception of fundraising by fans who donate the money to the club. Loans can also help out, but they have to be repaid at some time, so again, above-normal revenues will need to be realised, the amount depending on the rate of interest charged and the time period of the loan. Additionally, assets may be at risk if the finance companies insist on collateral for the loans. Assets could be liquidated to raise funds, but will there be a market for them? Probably not for players at that point in time but perhaps for ground facilities, though selling either of them might impair future performance. Some commentators have advocated for an expansion of equity capital, but share issue should really be for capital investment and creation of assets not to cover operating costs.

For an analytical discussion of how English football has tried to cope with the COVID-19 crisis, see Maguire (2021). He warns that any industry (to which I would add any club) which generates less revenue will have to find alternative income streams, cut its costs, rely on owner benevolence, or cease to exist.

At the grassroots level, the major expenditure comes from the players themselves in purchasing equipment, hiring facilities, and paying referees. All of these can be postponed so the impact is on manufacturers and suppliers (though continued production and stockpiling is feasible), councils and other landlords, and the unemployed match officials (likely to be part time anyway).

Can Sport Be Crisis Proofed?

That someone in Wuhan ate a bat or released a virus from a laboratory which ultimately closed down much of professional sport is an example of a spill-over effect which refers to the impact that seemingly unrelated events in one nation can have on the economies of other nations. Although there are positive spill-over effects, the term is most commonly applied to the negative impact a domestic event has on other parts of the world, such as an earthquake, stock market crisis, or another macro-event. It will happen again, but is the sports world prepared? If another politician tells me 'lessons will be learned', I will scream. But I am not a politician, so I can suggest what lessons might be learned to future-proof the sports sector from the worst effects of exogenous shocks to the economic system. These should be part of a general sustainability policy.

Revenue sharing is part and parcel of major leagues in the United States but has rarely been considered in Europe. However, some form of revenue redistribution from the richer clubs to those in need could help viability. This already occurs with parachute payments to relegated clubs and some contribution from the EPL to the lower leagues out of their broadcasting contract. During the pandemic, some leading Bundesliga clubs gave $20 million euros from their Champions League receipts to other clubs in divisions one and two (Drewes et al. 2021). The EPL has been reluctant to follow suit and assist those clubs in lower leagues (Grix et al. 2021). Yet they could well afford to do so: in 1990, average revenues in Division Four of the Football League were 12% of those clubs in the top division, but by 2015, although the names of the divisions had changed, the figure was just 2% (Reade and

Singleton 2020). Without altruism or enlightened self-interest, the gap will continue to widen, and the football family may turn out to be a dysfunctional one.

We need to know if clubs are living within their means. Far too many European football clubs consider reserves as those players on the substitute's bench rather than financial backup and have preferred to spend money on strengthening their squads rather than building up a contingency fund. In a case study of English football, Wilson et al. (2013) found 13 of the 21 clubs examined had experienced financial trouble, which suggests that they had not been accumulating surpluses as reserves for a rainy day but had been risking unsustainability by spending too much of their income in the search for improved playing performance. Economists have devised analytical tools (revolving around various financial ratios) to spot a club's potential for financial distress, but currently, no one in positions of responsibility in sport seems to want to know (Plumley et al. 2021).

The introduction of a (renewable) licensing system might force clubs to hold sufficient reserves to ride out a financial crisis. There is a precursor in that the German Football League introduced a licensing system which included an assessment of economic performance. This, it is argued, has successfully prevented any club from filing for insolvency during a season (Drewes et al. 2021). This contrasts with the English scenario outlined by Szymanski. Indeed, on the eve of the pandemic, the majority of English professional football clubs were on the brink of insolvency (Reade and Singleton 2020). Such a licensing system might force clubs to become less spendthrift. At the lower league levels, players may have to go part time or perhaps become part of the gig economy and be paid a match fee only.

Or should sport just gamble on the public purse being opened? Surely, no government would dare allow the modern opiate of the masses to fail. Banking was saved, so why not sport? We know that during the COVID-19 pandemic, governments worldwide treated elite sport more favourably than other branches of popular culture. However, that largesse tended to be regulatory rather than financial. Preserving grassroots sport might be more expensive and more problematic. The grassroots sports sector is often considered as important in improving the health and well-being of communities, solving societal issues, including reducing health inequalities, tackling obesity, cutting crime, easing loneliness, and enhancing social cohesion. Economists need to provide evidence to support these claims to pressure governments and non-government agencies to underwrite grassroots sport in an emergency.

References

Andersson, Karin, Sara Karlén, Jens Radmann and Susanna Hedenborg (2020), 'Voices from Closed Stadiums: The Corona Crisis as a Potential Vehicle for Sports Development', *Idrottsforum*, 20 November 2020.

Andreff, Wladamir (2006), 'Sports Accounting' in Wladamir Andreff and Stefan Szymanski (eds.), *Handbook on the Economics of Sport* (Edward Elgar: Cheltenham), 11–21.

Andreff, Wladimir (2010), 'Public and Private Sports Financing in Europe: The Impact of Financial Crisis', presentation at *18th European Association of Sports Management Conference* (Prague).

Henley Centre (1986), *The Economic Impact and Importance of Sport in the United Kingdom* (Sports Council: London).

Drewes, Michael, Frank Daumann and Florian Follert (2021), 'Exploring the Sports Economic Impact of COVID-19 on Professional Soccer', *Soccer and Society* 22.1–2, 125–137.

Grix, Jonathan, Paul Michael Brannagan, Holly Grimes and Ross Neville (2021), 'The Impact of Covid-19 on Sport', *International Journal of Sport Policy and Politics* 13.1, 1–12.

Horky, Thomas (2021), 'No Sports, No Spectators – No Media, No Money? The Importance of Spectators and Broadcasting for Professional Sports During COVID-19', *Soccer and Society* 22.1–2, 96–102.

Humphreys, Brad R. (2010), 'The Impact of the Global Financial Crisis on Sport in North America' in Sergiy Butenko, Jaime Gil-Lafuente and Panos M. Pardalos (eds.), *Optimal Strategies in Sports Economics and Management* (Springer-Verlag: Berlin), 39–57.

Mackreth, Kacy and Alexander John Bond (2020), 'Changing the Sport Product: Marketing Implications for Championship Rugby League Clubs in the United Kingdom', *Managing Sport and Leisure*, DOI: 10.1080/23750472.2020.1773298.

Maguire, Kieran (2021), *The Price of Football* (Agenda: Newcastle).

Plumley, Daniel, Jean-Philippe Serbera and Rob Wilson (2021), 'Too Big to Fail: Accounting for Prediction of Financial Distress in English Professional Football Clubs', *Journal of Applied Accounting* 22.1, 93–113.

Quansah, Tommy, Bernd Frick, Markus Lang and Kieran Maguire (2020), 'The Impact of the Coronavirus (COVID 19) on Player Salaries, Transfer Fees and Net Transfer Expenses in the English Premier League', *Social Science Research Network*, DOI: 10.13140/RG.2.2.36761.24160

Reade, J. James and Carl Singleton (2020), 'European Football After COVID-19', in Monica Billio and Simone Varotto (eds.), *A New World Post COVID-19: Lessons for Business, the Finance Industry and Policy Makers* (Ca' Foscari University Press: Venice), 349–358.

Research Nester, *Sports Good Market: Global Demand Analysis and Opportunity Outlook*, 8 April 2020.

Rogstad, Egil Trasti (2020), 'Virtual Light in the Sports Blackout', *Idrottsforum*, 20 October 2008.

Sánchez, Luis Carlos, Ángel Barajas and Patricio Sánchez-Fernández (2019), 'Sport Finance' in Jaume Garcia Villar (ed.), *Sport (and) Economies* (Nisan: Madrid), 327–367.

Schmal, Benedikt (2021), 'The Long Shadow of an Infection: COVID-19 and Performance at Work', Discussion Paper University of Reading Economics of Sport Online Seminar (3 September).

Szymanski, Stefan (2001), 'Economics of Sport: Introduction', *Economic Journal* 2001, F1–F3.

Szymanski, Stefan (2010), 'The Financial Crisis and English Football: The Dog That Will Not Bark', *International Journal of Sport Finance* 5.1, 28–40.

Tan, Tien-Chin and Jung Woo Lee (2020), 'Covid-19 and Sport in the Asia Pacific Region', *Sport in Society* 23.12, 1883–1888.

Terrien, Mickael, Bastien Du Fau, Yann Carnin and Wladimir Andreff (2021), 'Economic Models of French Amateur Soccer Clubs. From One Crisis to the Other: Which Transformation?', *Journal of Global Sport Management*, DOI: 10.1080/24704067.2021.1910060.

Thibault, Lucie (2014), 'Sport and Management Studies' in Joseph Maguire (ed.), *Social Sciences in Sport* (Human Kinetics: Champaign, IL), 305–340.

Wilson, Robert, Daniel Plumley and Girish Ramchandani (2013), 'The Relationship between Ownership Structure and Club Performance in the English Premier League', *Sport, Business and Management* 3.1, 19–36.

INDEX

Printed in the United States
by Baker & Taylor Publisher Services